Beginning Android Tablet Games Programming

Jeremy Kerfs

Apress®

Beginning Android Tablet Games Programming

ISBN-13 (pbk): 978-1-4302-3852-2

ISBN-13 (electronic): 978-1-4302-3853-9

President and Publisher: Paul Manning
Lead Editor: Steve Anglin and Michelle Lowman
Technical Reviewer: Jelani John
Editorial Board: Steve Anglin, Mark Beckner, Ewan Buckingham, Gary Corne ll, Morgan Ertel, Jonathan Gennick, Jonathan Hasse ll, Robe rt Hutchin son, Mich elle Lowman, Jame s Markham, Mat thew Moodie , Je ff O lson, Jeffrey P epper, Douglas Pu ndick, Be n R enow-Clarke, D ominic Shakeshaft, G wenan Sp earing, Matt Wa de, Tom Welsh
Coordinating Editor: Anita Castro
Copy Editor: Tiffany Taylor
Compositor: Bytheway Publishing Services
Indexer: SPI Global
Artist: SPI Global
Cover Designer: Anna Ishchenko

Distributed to the book trade worldwide by Springer Scie nce+Business Media New York, 233 Spring Street, 6th Floor, New York, NY 10013. Phone 1-800-SPRINGER, f ax (20 1) 348 -4505, e-mail orders-ny@springer-sbm.com, or v isit www.springeronline.com.

For information on translations, please e-mail rights@apress.com, or visit www.apress.com.

Apress and friends of ED book s may be purchased in bulk f or academic, corporate, or promo tional use. eBoo k versions and licenses are also available for most ti tles. For more information, reference our Special Bulk Sales–eBook Licensing web page at www.apress.com/bulk-sales.

Any source code or other supplementary materials ref erenced by the author i n this te xt is av ailable to re aders at www.apress.com. For detailed inf ormation about how to lo cate your book's source code, go t o www.apress.com/source-code/.

Contents at a Glance

Contents

About the Author

 **Jeremy Kerfs** is a technical writer for various robotics and consumer-technology magazines. He has taught basic computer science classes for children, and he continues to work as a web development consultant. His passion for entrepreneurship and programming led him to recently create Laughing Studios with the goal of developing mobile games and applications.

He keeps his sanity by playing the piano and running. When there is a strong enough breeze, he will be windsurfing on the San Francisco bay.

About the Technical Reviewer

 **Jelani John** is a freelance developer and animator from Brooklyn. He enjoys making games and playing with new technologies. You can find him at www.jelanijohn.com.

Acknowledgments

Frank Pohlmann, Editorial Director at Apress, gave me the tremendous opportunity to write this book. I am very grateful for your advice and coaching as we hashed out what the book would look like.

A very special thanks to Anita Castro, the coordinating editor, who pushed me through the sometimes arduous task of completing the chapters, graphics, and code for this book. You gave me some incredible advice and were very patient with me throughout the process.

Thank you to all of the editors and reviewers who worked on the project with me. Your technical advice, wordsmithing, and organizational ideas made this book immeasurably better.

I have also had many great mentors and colleagues who prompted me to do what I thought was impossible. Thank you to Dave Briccetti for introducing me to the art of teaching computer science. Paul Spinrad was an amazing editor for *Make Magazine* who inspired me to take on this project after I read his two stunning books. Paul gave me good pointers, was patient with me, and refused to get angry despite my fickleness. I am very grateful to you.

Setting Up Android 3.0 Java Development

This book teaches you to create your own games for Android 3.0 tablets. After reading and working through its examples, you'll have gained command over the sensors, touchscreen, network capabilities, and processing power of the many new tablet computers. Does that sound daunting? It isn't. Instead of going through the drudgery of developing stodgy corporate apps that locate a store or present a coupon, you'll know how to make fun and intriguing games. If you've done some game development in the past, you may be pleasantly surprised to learn how simple the Android system makes this process when compared to traditional PC and console game development.

Although no book ever written can take you from newbie to game programming guru, the foundation presented in this book will let you make any of your 2D game ideas into a reality. This book makes the programming as simple as possible in order to concentrate on the more creative aspects of game development.

What Is Android?

Android is very special, and you'll gain much more appreciation for it as you get into the programming. The movement of many handset makers to create tablets running the Android OS created a huge market for the games you'll make. This section gives you a rundown of Android's features and history.

The Beginnings of Android

In 2003, Android began as a small Silicon Valley startup company with the aim to create a more interactive and helpful interface for smartphones. Google quickly snatched up the company in 2005 as part of its push to enter the mobile phone market. After Google acquired it, the first Android OS was soon released during 2007. In subsequent years, Android went through many revisions (more than seven major changes) that made it one of the leading operating systems for smartphones, with some saying that Android has nearly 50% of mobile devices.

The revisions to Android are very important to understanding how development works. Google worked hard to ensure backward compatibility in its version of Android; however, applications generally are designed to work for a select couple of Android editions to guarantee the best performance and user experience. The version called Froyo is still the most popular for developers, but the later versions are gaining steam as more modern devices like tablets require more powerful operating systems.

The following list of Android versions, along with their current market share, illustrates which versions remain popular and therefore are of interest to developers. The creative name given to each version by Google is next to the edition number. Developers often go by these names rather than merely the numbers. Keep in mind that with the exception of Android 3.0, all versions of the OS were designed for phones exclusively:

- Android 1.5 Cupcake (2.3%)

- Android 1.6 Donut (3.0%)

- Android 2.1 Éclair (24.5%)

- Android 2.2 Froyo (65.9%)

- Android 2.3 Gingerbread (1.0%)

- Android 2.3.3 Gingerbread (3.0%)

- Android 3.0 Honeycomb (0.3%)

If you're interested in checking the current market share of the various versions, go to http://developer.android.com/resources/dashboard/platform-versions.html.

After examining this list, many would say that you should be making games for Froyo because it has a huge lead in market share over other versions. The reason for Froyo's prevalence is that it's installed on many simpler older phones that can only get updated versions through a complicated process. These devices will slowly become inconsequential as the newer versions take center stage. To some extent, making games for the majority of users makes sense; however, every day new users are buying more modern phones that use the later versions. Also, perhaps the most important point is that hundreds of thousands of apps are playable on the Froyo version, and it's increasingly difficult to stand out.

With that being said, this book teaches you to designs games for the latest edition (Honeycomb) for two reasons. First, Honeycomb is the only version optimized for tablets, which are much more immersive and fun than any smartphone. Second, Android tablet computing is growing at a huge rate as more companies release tablets that can compete with Apple's iPad. With the failure of webOS, Android and iOS are the only contenders in the tablet market. Microsoft has also come out with its own operating system, but it has not yet garnered significant market share. Google's often-quoted statement about 500,000 Android devices being registered each day gives you a sense of how fast this market is expanding.

Android 3.0 Features

Honeycomb is a huge advance from the previous Android versions. Designed to utilize a much larger screen and more powerful processor, Android 3.0 lets developers expand their usually modest smartphone games. Many of the new features are user-interface changes that make the desktop accessible to users with a screen that is several times bigger than a smartphone screen. For example, typical phones have two- to three-inch screens, whereas tablets boast impressive nine- to ten-inch screens. These updates are convenient; however, game developers concentrate more on the updates to speedier graphics rendering and the new sensors and network abilities of the operating system.

Not all games use all of these features, but it's crucial to consider their importance in designing unique games. The larger screen is in itself an update worth noting. The high-resolution screens demand artwork that is scalable and visually appealing. Many Android tablets have landed on 1280×800 as their screen size. This is comparable to the resolution that many computer screens still use. In this case, the graphics must approximate the images used in computer games.

Table 1-1 list major changes to Android 3.0 of particular interest to game developers.

Table 1-1. Android 3.0 Features

Updates to Android 3.0	Relevance to Game Development
3D user interface design	Games and apps can use new themes that provide a quick and professional look with minimal work.
Better desktop widgets	Multiplayer games allow users to make simple changes right on the desktop.
Powerful graphics capabilities	Games can use more realistic high-resolution images without losing out on fast performance.
Multicore processor support	All aspects of a game can be speeded up by allocating different routines to separate cores.
Customizable action bar	Some games may find the bar at the top of the app useful for providing updates or posting scores and points.
Notification and system bar	Although this isn't truly a game-oriented update, it can be useful for letting users monitor any changes or updates in a game.
Bluetooth connectivity changes	Devices like joysticks and keyboards can now be readily connected to tablets for a new user-input method.

Throughout the book, I give advice about how to make the most of the new Android tablet features. If you're looking to make games as a hobby by yourself, then watch for my notes about where to get quality sounds and images royalty-free. The tools I use for making music and graphics for my games are also explained in depth later in chapter 2.

I hope that after getting acquainted with Android, you're ready to get started. Read the next section carefully, though, to ensure that you have the proper skills and hardware to develop games for Android.

What You Need to Create Android Games

So what does it take to become an Android games developer? Let's look at the skills you need to get the most from this book and the system you need to work through its examples.

What You Need to Know

How hard is programming Android games? This really depends on how experienced you are with Java and the Android operating system. If you have a solid knowledge of Java, then you'll be perfectly at home with this book. If you've written code for Android before, then you may not be challenged by any of the code here and are free to enjoy the experience as you go. Read this section carefully before proceeding, so you know exactly what you need.

Generally, people interested in learning to create games for tablets in Android come from three different backgrounds. Each background prepares you for the examples in this book, but they all require a slightly different approach.

If you know both Java and Android, you're ready to go. The code here resembles what you've seen before, but it focuses on graphics, game loops, and rapid responses to user input that you may not have dealt with. Regardless of what you've done, this book helps you master the creation of tablet games.

Maybe you're comfortable with Java, but you've never worked with Android. This is fine. You won't have much difficulty working through the examples and code. Remember that with any new environment and API, you should regularly look up the functions and classes that are presented. Becoming familiar with Android takes time, but it's well worth the effort.

You may never have coded so much as an if statement in Java, much less worked with Android. If this is the case, you can still use this book, but you have to get a Java primer. I strongly recommend *Learn Java for Android Development* by Jeff Friesen (Apress, 2010). When you have a reference for Java, become familiar with how Java works, and then jump right into this text. You learn the language as you go through it.

An understanding of XML is beneficial; however, XML is relatively simple to understand, and you should have no problem dealing with this book's relatively elementary use of it. With the qualifications out of the way, it's time to consider the environment used for game creation.

What You Need for a Platform

It's time to get your hands dirty and find out what you actually need for developing Android games. Fortunately, you shouldn't have to buy any software! The only expense is a $25 registration fee when you're ready to put your games on the Android Market. First, check to make sure your computer will support Android development:

- Windows XP (32-bit), Vista (32- or 64-bit), or Windows 7 (32- or 64-bit)

- Mac OS X 10.5.8 or later (x86 only)

- Linux (tested on Ubuntu Linux, Lucid Lynx)

This list was compiled from Android's own system requirements. Check http://developer.android.com/sdk/requirements.html for the most recent changes to minimum system standards.

Although a system that meets the minimum requirements will let you create Android applications, testing your programs may be rather slow. Generally, if you can play modern video games on your computer, then you should be fine. However, if you have a slower machine, don't despair; you'll be perfectly capable of writing Android games, but you should test them on an Android tablet rather than a simulator on your computer.

You don't need an Android tablet to complete any exercise or program in this book, but there is no substitute for testing your creations on a real device. With a glut of tablets on the market, cheaper models will set you back about $500 to $700. These are well worth the investment if you find game programming as addicting as I do. Motorola and Samsung make some of the most popular tablets; look for their offerings to see the top of the line in terms of Android tablets.

If you're confident in your skills and have decided on which machine you want to plunge into game development, you're ready to acquire your tools and configure your development environment.

Setting Up Your Android Tablet Programming Environment

You're nearly at the fun part, but first you must make sure your computer is properly set up. You must download and install three packages for your work:

- Java Development Kit (JDK)

- Eclipse, which is the integrated development environment (IDE)

- Android Java SDK

If you're a Java developer, then you likely have a recent version of the JDK and probably even have Eclipse installed. In that case, skip to the Android SDK portion of the following instructions. Look over the first two sections if you experience problems, though, because you may be using the wrong version of the JDK or Eclipse.

In the following sections, you work through installing each of these packages. When you're done, you'll be ready to create your first Android tablet program. This entire process shouldn't take more than 20 minutes before you're ready to go.

Installing the Java JDK

The first step is to download and install the latest version of the JDK for your machine. Here's how:

1. To find the JDK you need for your system, go to
   www.oracle.com/technetwork/java/javase/downloads/index.html. You need
   the JDK to let you use the Java language on your computer. Look for the large
   Java icon at upper left on the page, and select the JDK link, as labeled in Figure
   1-1. This link takes you to the JDK SE downloads page.

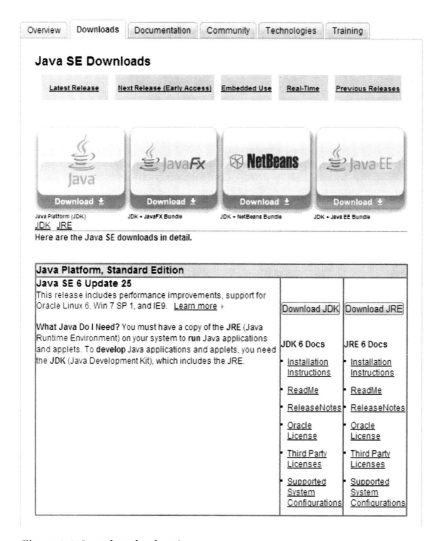

Figure 1-1. *Java download options page*

2.   On the Downloads tab of the Java SE Downloads page, shown in Figure 1-2, accept the license agreement, choose the package that fits your operating system, and click the link to download it.

Figure 1-2. License agreement and Java version selection

3. When the file downloads, run the installer. On some computers, the installer starts automatically. If this doesn't happen, locate the folder where the files were downloaded, and sort the folder by the Date Modified. The last file is this installer. Double-click it, and you're ready to go.

4. When the welcome dialog page for Installation for Java wizard appears, as shown in Figure 1-3, click the Next button and follow the instructions provided by the wizard to finish the installation.

Figure 1-3. JDK installation wizard

Now you're ready to set up Eclipse, the development environment you use throughout this book to build your games. Without Eclipse, you would be forced to compile your code using a command line. A development environment saves you a lot of time.

Installing the Eclipse IDE

With the JDK installed, you can now set up your developer environment. You're going to use Eclipse, a free software package with lots of great support for Java and Android developers. Follow these steps:

1. To locate the Eclipse package for your system, go to
    www.eclipse.org/downloads/. On the Eclipse Downloads page, shown in Figure
    1-4, use the small drop-down menu to match your operating system. Then
    select Eclipse IDE for Java Developers, and click the link for the version you
    need for your operating system. You're brought to a download page.

Figure 1-4. Eclipse download options page

2. Download the zipped folder that contains the version you've selected, and extract it. Click the install executable. During the installation, make sure you check the box that creates a shortcut to Eclipse on your desktop to enable us to easily access Eclipse later on.

3. When the installation is completed, you can start Eclipse via its shortcut. You should see something like Figure 1-5. This means everything is working.

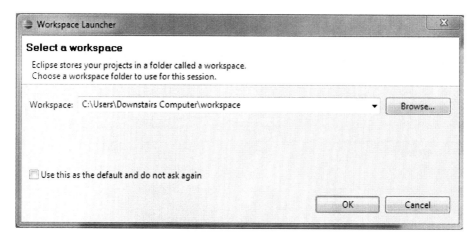

Figure 1-5. Eclipse as it's starting up

With your developer platform installed, you're ready to add the Android SDK, which provides you with the libraries and tools you need to start building games. So far, you've only worked on the basics, which include the Java language and the development environment.

Installing the Android SDK

The last package you need for your platform is Google's Android SDK:

1. To locate the package you need for your system, go to
    http://developer.android.com/sdk/index.html, shown in Figure 1-6, and
    select the Android SDK package that is made for your operating system by
    clicking its link. When you've done this, the appropriate file begins
    downloading.

Figure 1-6. The Android SDK download page

2. When the folder or installer is downloaded, run it by finding the file and double-clicking it. The Welcome page of the Android SDK Tools Setup Wizard appears, as shown in Figure 1-7.

Figure 1-7. The Android SDK setup wizard

▓ **Note** Remember the location where you install the SDK. I prefer to use `C:\Android\android_sdk\`. Make a note of the place where it's installed regardless of which operating system you're using. We will need its location in the steps to come when we are connecting it to Eclipse.

3. Click the Next button, and follow the wizard's instructions to install the SDK. Eventually, you reach the last page. The Start SDK Manager check box should be selected, as shown in Figure 1-8. This causes the SDK Manager to start immediately after the installation is complete.

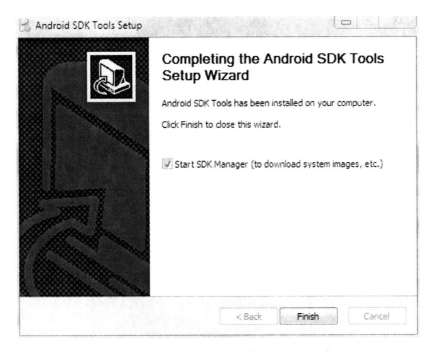

Figure 1-8. *The end of the Android SDK Tools Setup Wizard.*

4. When the Android SDK and AVD Manager dialog opens, as shown in Figure 1-9, click the Available Packages link in the left navigation panel, and then click the Install Selected button. This step accepts and installs the default Android packages recommended by Google that you use for games. Without installing these, you can't use several tools and sample apps.

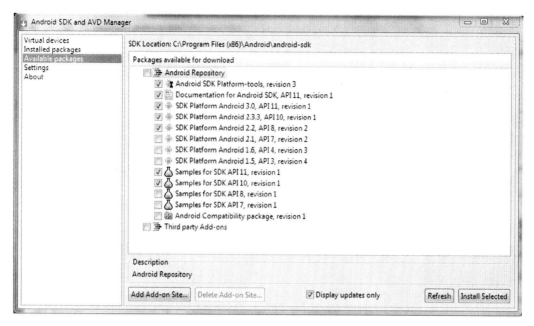

Figure 1-9. The Android SDK Manager. Note the default packages selected.

5. When you click Install Selected, a dialog box like the one shown in Figure 1-10 appears, to show the progress of the installation (this may take several minutes).

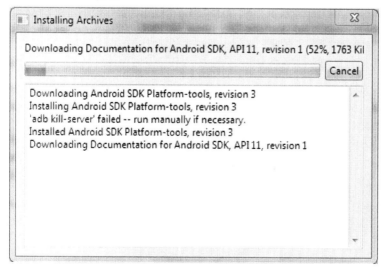

Figure 1-10. The installation of the packages and archives

Now you have the Java language, the development environment, and the Android tools. The only step left is to integrate all these parts together.

Adding Android Tools and a Virtual Device to Eclipse

The last work you have to do is getting Eclipse to mesh with the new Android tools and programs. Doing so lets you type your code into Eclipse and then test from Eclipse itself. Otherwise, you'd have to save your code and use a different program to test the app. Follow these steps:

1. To equip your copy of Eclipse with the Android tools you'll be using, open Eclipse and select Help   Install New Software. An Eclipse Install dialog appears, as shown in Figure 1-11. You return to this Install dialog every time you need to add more functionality to Eclipse.

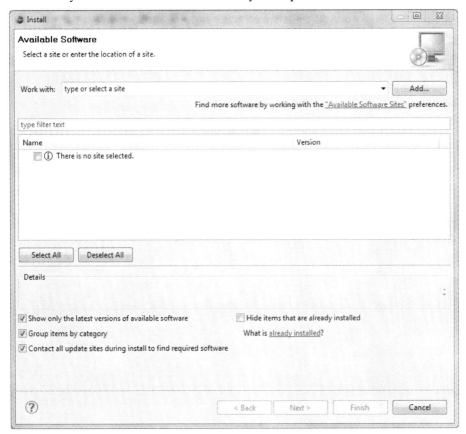

Figure 1-11. The install dialog box for Eclipse.

2. You first need to let Eclipse know where to look for the tools you want to add. On the Install screen, click the Add button at upper right. An Add Repository dialog opens, as shown in Figure 1-12.

Figure 1-12. The Name and Location boxes used to add Android tools to Eclipse

3. Do the following:

a. In the Name box, type **Android Tools**, which is the name you'll use to refer to the tools this step installs.

b. For a Location, enter the URL **https://dl-ssl.google.com/android/eclipse/**, which is the location of the tools you're adding.

4. When you've finished, click the OK button, which returns you to the Install dialog shown in Figure 1-13.

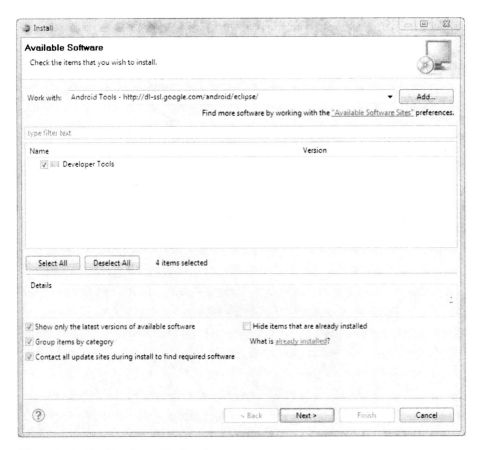

Figure 1-13. The Developer Tools software

5. Select the Developer Tools check box, and follow the prompts to install the updates. Doing so adds the tools you need for Android tablet development.

6. Restart Eclipse when the dialog box prompts you to do so.

7. In Eclipse, select Window Preferences. Open the Android tab on the side pane. Your screen should look like Figure 1-14. You're about to point Eclipse to the installation of your Android SDK. This lets you compile the programs from within Eclipse.

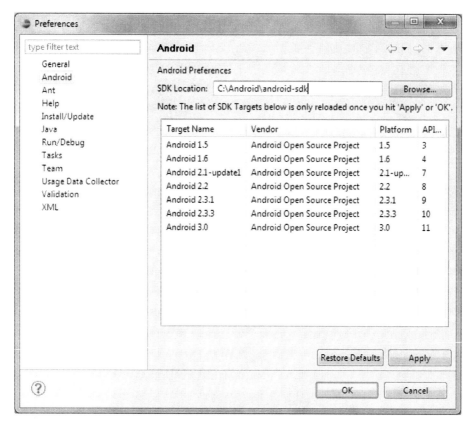

Figure 1-14. The configuration options for Android in Eclipse.

8. Type the exact name of the location where you downloaded the Android SDK in the SDK Location field. My example uses C:\Android\Android-sdk.

When you've applied these changes, you're done with the setup process!

From now on, you focus on the structure of actual Android apps and how to make your visions for a game come true. This background makes it easy for you to try out a variety of different tools and techniques in your games. Being able to quickly change your code and see the result of your efforts is invaluable in your efforts.

Putting Your Tools to the Test

By now, you're probably eagerly anticipating some tangible Android games. This section goes over how to use the tools you've installed to play with Android's built-in library of sample programs. It also introduces the basics of designing an application's appearance. Future chapters expand on these projects to make a full-featured game.

Each of your Android games will be developed as an Eclipse project that holds all of its images, sounds, and code in one location. You'll gain a better understanding of Eclipse as you go. Understanding the storage of resources and how you access files in this environment is a critical skill you work on.

The sample programs are a terrific resource for even the most advanced programmer. Much of the basic functionality you need for any game you write has already been implemented in one or more of these programs and is most likely available for free. A cursory look online can save you dozens of hours of work in the future. Sadly, most of the apps are written for older versions of Android, so they appear very small on a large tablet screen. To compensate, you can incorporate some of their code into your projects but handle the graphics yourself.

In the rest of this section, you walk through the steps of creating an Android game for the tablet. It's important to start from scratch at least once so you can see the most basic framework of a game. You begin by creating your first Android project with Eclipse.

Creating an Android Project

The first step in building any Android game is to create an Eclipse project:

1. In Eclipse, select File New Project, select Android Project under the Android folder, and move on to the New Android Project screen, shown in Figure 1-15.

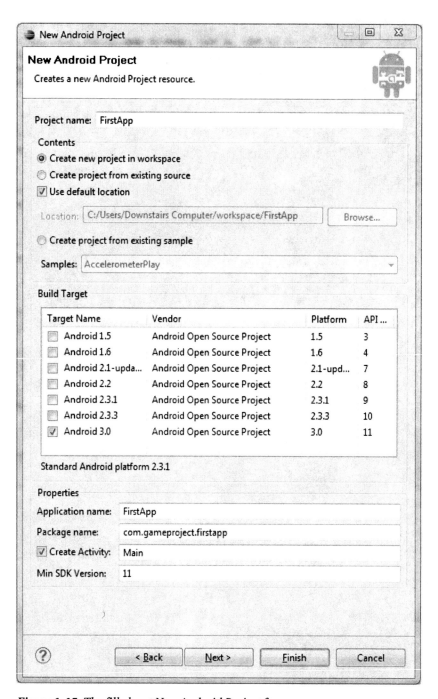

Figure 1-15. The filled-out New Android Project form

2. Fill in the missing information:

   a. Type the name **FirstApp** or any name you wish for the Project Name.

   b. Leave the other sections unchanged from the defaults until you get to the Build Target section. Here is where you decide what version of Android you would like your app built for. Select Android 3.0, because you want your application to run on the latest tablet computers. This designation becomes crucial when you're testing your game, and you want to make sure it runs well on a simulated tablet rather than the small screen of a phone.

   c. Application Name is generally the same as Project Name for your purposes. Retype **FirstApp** or the name you used for the project.

   d. The Package Name field will be familiar to Java developers, but it may be confusing if you aren't familiar with it. Here you declare the name as `com.gameproject.firstapp`.

   Packages are Java's means of organizing code to make it easy to use previously written files. You can read more about Java packages at `http://java.sun.com/docs/books/jls/third_edition/html/packages.html`, but it isn't terrifically important for you right now. You revisit this when you're ready to share your apps with the world later.

   e. Write **Main** as the activity you want the project to create.

   Activities are essential to Android programs, and I go into more depth about them later. For now, think of this activity as the primary function of the app. It's called on to set up the game and then later run the game by processing input and directing the movement of sprites. Activities should be named based on their role, so the original activity is usually called Main, MainActivity, or something similar.

   f. Fill in the Min SDK Version field with the number **11**. This means Android requires devices to be running Android version 11 in order to properly run your game.

   You're probably curious why I suddenly jumped to the number 11, when I previously talked about Android 3.0 as the latest update. Well, Android has a crazy system of naming versions. The level 3.0 refers to the platform version, which follows the normal software convention where small updates increase the tenths place, and a major revision gets a new number. To be consistent, Android associates a code with each platform version. Android 3.0 is assigned 11, where Android 2.3.3 got 10. Because your project is made for the latest edition of Android, you type **11** as the minimum SDK version.

3. Figure 1-15 shows a completed New Android Project form. Check yours to make sure it's the same, because the remaining code and examples use the names provided in this walkthrough. When you're done, click Finish. You're brought to a blank Eclipse screen with a folder for your project on the far left.

Now let's take a look at the files and code that Eclipse creates.

Exploring the Android Project in Eclipse

To see what files were created with the project, expand the FirstApp folder. Then further expand src to com.gameproject.firstapp to Main.java. Double-click Main.java to show the file in Eclipse editor (the large viewing pane in the center). This is the meat of your game; however, currently it's a basic skeleton. The code you see should look like the code in Listing 1-1.

Listing 1-1. Main.java

```
package com.gameproject.firstapp;

import android.app.Activity;
import android.os.Bundle;

public class Main extends Activity {
    /** Called when the activity is first created. */
    @Override
    public void onCreate(Bundle savedInstanceState) {
        super.onCreate(savedInstanceState);
        setContentView(R.layout.main);
    }
}
```

The code in Listing 1-1 creates a new class and then has the class update the view that the user sees. The first three lines define the package and then import the classes that the app needs to use. Note that both imports refer to classes that are parts of the Android SDK. As you make more functional games, you'll import many other classes that let you perform a variety of actions.

Let's take a closer look at the code in the listing line by line:

```
package com.gameproject.firstapp
```

This simple introduction specifies that this file is part of the firstapp package. Packages are the way that Java groups files that are for the same program.

```
import android.app.Activity;
import android.os.Bundle;
```

Import statements add functionality to your project. In reality, these are other packages that you want to use. Activity includes the methods that handle the running of the app. Bundle is a specific way of storing information for your app.

```
public class Main extends Activity
```

Here, the class Main is given all the functions and variables that the Android class Activity had. Whenever a class extends another, the new class inherits or receives access to all of the other class's functionality.

```
public void onCreate(Bundle savedInstanceState)
```

The function defined here is actually from the Activity class. It handles all the procedures that must be completed upon the startup of the application. The Bundle argument, savedInstanceState, holds the previous status of the application. When you start the app for the first time, it's null.

```
super.onCreate(savedInstanceState);
```

The onCreate method of the Activity class is called. This causes the program to start the app. Notice the keyword super in front of the function. The super keyword means that the program is calling the original onCreate method from the Android SDK, not the new onCreate method that you created in the line before.

SetContentView(R.layout.main);

Finally, the application does its first real task by setting the Android screen to an XML file. R is an identifier that means *resource*, layout specifies what type of resource, and main refers to the name of the file. Shortly you edit the main.xml file to change the appearance of the program.

It's time to run the program and find out what it does. Before you do this, though, you must create a virtual Android device to test it on. If you have an Android tablet running Android 3.0, you can test the program directly on it. To learn how to do this, go to Appendix A.

Creating a Virtual Android Device

Creating your own virtual device is a very simple process in Eclipse:

1. On the Eclipse main menu bar, select Window Android SDK and AVD Manager. An Android SDK and AVD Manager screen like the one shown earlier in Figure 1-8 opens.

2. Because you don't have any devices listed, click the New button at upper left. A Create New Android Virtual Device (AVD) dialog box pops up to let you define your new simulator, as shown in Figure 1-16. Complete the form as follows:

    a. The name of the device doesn't matter; I chose the uncreative name **Tablet_device**.

    b. The target Android version for you is Android 3.0.

    c. For most applications, you don't need to worry about the size of the SD card. However, if you make a game that requires you to store high scores or other data on the device, specify the size of the onboard data storage.

    d. The Skin and Hardware sections don't need to be changed. It's interesting to note the hardware specifications, though. When you make graphics for a game, you should definitely use an LCD density of 160 (which is fairly standard) to determine the resolution of your images. The device RAM size of the simulator is actually fairly low compared to many tablets. However, the simulator doesn't accurately represent RAM or processor power. For a real representation of how your game will run, you must try it on a real device.

Figure 1-16. Creating an Android Virtual Device (AVD)

3.   Click the Create AVD button, and you're ready to run your app.

If you're expecting a simulator to pop up, you'll be disappointed; the new virtual device only starts when you run your application. The next section starts the device.

Running the App

Follow these quick steps to run the application:

1.   In the center of the toolbar near the top of the Eclipse screen is a green Play button. Click it, and your program should open a large black screen. This is your new simulator. For a while, the screen displays the word *Android* as it loads. Then the word *Android* in a larger font scrolls up as the loading is completed.

2. When the loading screens are finished, move the small circular knob to the right. If you wait long enough, the app may start automatically. In this case, the words *Hello World, Main!* appear. If not, go to the next step.

3. The home screen comes up with a Google search bar at upper left and a couple of buttons at the bottom. A real device uses touch gestures to select apps, but the simulator lets you use your mouse cursor. To run your own program, click the Apps icon at upper right on the screen.

4. A list of all the programs on the device appears. Your app has the generic Android robot as its icon; the app name (FirstApp) appears under the icon. Click it, and the screen soon reads Hello World, Main!

As simple as it may be, you've launched your first Android application. When you're done reveling in it, click the arrow at lower left pointing toward the left side of the screen. You're back at the desktop home. Try out some of the other apps in the simulator now. You may be surprised to see that the browser, e-mail, and other programs do exactly what you would expect.

The AVD is very similar to the real thing, even allowing you to test sensors and GPS data. To put this emulator through its paces, you can make your own incredible apps. Take a look at the next section to see how you can work with your code.

Making Your First Changes to the App

Although you did technically create your own app, you haven't had to manipulate the code beyond what was automatically created. Now it's time to change the text of the program:

1. In the project's folder tree, expand the Res folder.

2. Open the values folder. You should find a single file there (strings.xml); double-click it to show it in the viewing pane.

3. Two string resources are listed. One is the app name, and the other is named hello. Click hello, and change the value to any string you want.

4. Save your changes and rerun the program. When you open FirstApp, you should see that you've changed the text on the screen.

To understand how this worked, you need to know about the important Android topic of *resources*. The strings.xml file that you just edited is a resource. The same is true of every file within the large Res folder.

If you remember from the main.java file, I mentioned one resource file in the code: main.xml, in the layout section. You have some changes to make to this file:

5. To view the file, expand the layout folder and double-click main.xml. A WYSIWYG editor appears with a small screen and the string you created at upper right.

6. Unfortunately, the screen was designed for a cell phone. You can change this quickly by using the menu with 2.7in QVGA at the top. Scroll down through the list until you reach 10.1 WXGA. This makes a screen layout of a little more than ten inches, which is normal for a tablet.

7. Updating the layout is very easy with the editor. The pane on the left already has several different items that can be dragged onto the app. Try putting a button right beneath the text you wrote.

8. Although the WYSIWYG editor is convenient, it isn't extremely useful for making games. You need to get into the actual file behind the image. To see this, click main.xml (near the bottom of the screen, next to Graphical Layout).

Listing 1-2 shows the code you should see after you add a button to the layout.

Listing 1-2. Main.xml

```
<?xml version="1.0" encoding="utf-8"?>
<LinearLayout xmlns:android="http://schemas.android.com/apk/res/android"
    android:orientation="vertical"
    android:layout_width="fill_parent"
    android:layout_height="fill_parent"
    android:id="@+id/Button">
<TextView
    android:layout_width="fill_parent"
    android:layout_height="wrap_content"
    android:text="@string/hello"
    />
<Button  android:text="Button"
        android:id="@+id/button1"
        android:layout_width="wrap_content"
        android:layout_height="wrap_content">
        </Button>
</LinearLayout>
```

If you aren't familiar with XML, then this may look like Greek, but it's actually very easy to understand. The first line is a declaration of what type of XML you're using. The next section creates a special layout type called a LinearLayout. Within this, simple instructions tell the device how to orient the app and what size it should be relative to the entire device screen. Next a TextView object is created to fill_parent (expand to fit the whole space) and then defined to wrap_content, which limits the view to only the amount necessary.

Finally, text is inserted into the screen by calling on the string resource entitled hello. This is the hello string that you already edited.

The next section is the Button information that you dragged onto your app. It's important to recall that XML layouts don't create functionality, merely the appearance of the program. For example, clicking your button doesn't do anything unless you specifically program a response to it.

Summary

This chapter definitely covered a lot of ground in terms of getting your development environment up and running. You covered the concepts behind Android and how you go about creating games. In the next chapters, you thoroughly examine layouts and how to create an attractive background for a game. Then you create sprites and start adding some flavor to your apps by moving players around the screen. Later chapters add user input, sounds, and AI to finish off your creations.

CHAPTER 2

Creating Simple Games with Sprites and Movement

Congratulations—you've successfully set up your development environment and are ready to move on to the more creative activities of game development. When you think of your favorite game, you can immediately conjure up what the appearance of it was, whether it included monsters running toward you or cars racing around a track. In this chapter, you breathe life into your tablet screen. With tons of games on the market, the way your game looks and feels can determine how successful it is.

This chapter covers the basics of displaying images to the tablet screen and then moving them around. You learn about the notion of *sprites*. For the purposes of this chapter, a sprite is any game object that can be moved around during game play. The main character in a game or one of its enemies is normally a sprite, but the game's background isn't.

The content in this chapter moves fairly quickly and introduces many new concepts.

Working with Images

Sprites are fundamental to games, and before you can create a game, you need to be able to draw its cards, characters, and other objects on the screen. In this section you will work with the fundamental components of graphic displays for Android 3.0. We will also work out the components of sprites and move our images across the screen. This will become the basis for our future projects. Take a look at Figure 2-1 to see what our game will look like. This start sprite is actually bouncing back and forth.

Figure 2-1. The completed Graphics Program.

■ **Note** If you get lost, copy the code from the Google Code project connected to this book. Then go back to the lessons, and you'll be able to understand how the program works by manipulating aspects of it.

Creating a Image Display Surface

To get started, you need to open a new Eclipse project. In the last chapter, you created a new project in Eclipse entitled FirstApp. That code is no longer of any use to you. Start over with an entirely new project:

1. Select File New Project Android Project on the Eclipse main menu.

2. When the New Android Project dialog box appears, complete it. You probably remember this process from the previous examples, so feel free to fill out the form by yourself.

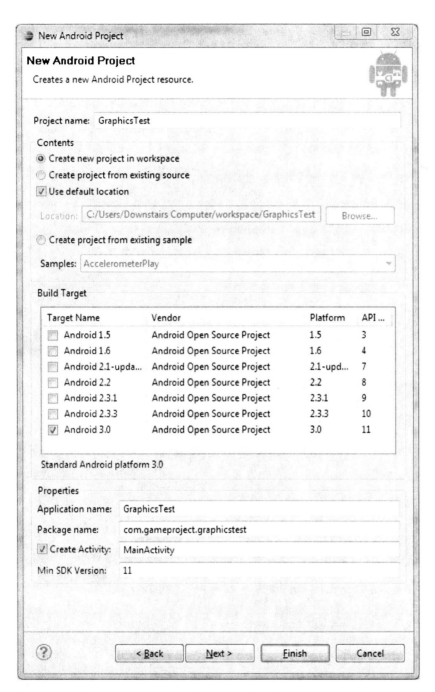

Figure 2-2. The project creation window for GraphicsTest..

3.   The name of your app is GraphicsTest. Make sure the completed form looks like the one shown in Figure 2-2. Getting used to making new projects in Eclipse is very important because it's often the easiest way to start over with a clean slate if something goes wrong.

4.   When the form is complete, click Finish. If you need help filling out the other fields, refer back to Chapter 1.

Before you can display images on a tablet, you need a canvas in which to render them. You build that surface in the main routine of your program. Follow these steps:

1.   The files from the first project are probably still open in your main editing panel. Close them by right-clicking next to the file tabs and selecting Close All. This doesn't delete the code, but rather closes the editing screens that display it.

2.   Open the file tree for the GraphicsTest project in the Eclipse Package Explorer (located at left onscreen). You want to examine the Java code, so open the src folder, and then continue expanding until you see MainActivity.java. Figure 2-3 shows where you find the files.

Figure 2-3. Package Explorer for GraphicsTest

3.   Open MainActivity.java in the editing pane, and you see the same generic code that you saw generated in the first chapter.

4.   In Chapter 1, you got by with a single file of Java code and an XML file to handle the layout. Sadly, a game that involves lots of movement and changing of graphics can't be readily built using XML. Therefore, you need a Java file that is dedicated to running the graphics for your game.

5.   To do this, create a new class by right-clicking com.gameproject.graphicstest in the GraphicsTest Package Explorer. Select New   Class. A dialog box opens

and asks what you want your new class to be called. Type **GameView**, and be careful to leave all the other fields with their default values. When you're done, you find two files (MainActivity and GameView) in your src directory.

6. Open the GameView.java file in the viewing pane. There you should find the code shown in Listing 2-1.

Listing 2-1. GameView.java

```
package com.gameproject.graphicstest;

public class GameView {

}
```

You add to this primitive source to draw an image file to the screen. Before you start this, however, you must learn the fundamentals of views and displays in Android.

How the Android View Class Works

So far, you've only used two Android classes in your projects: Activity and Bundle. Activities hold the functions that handle the creation, running, and closing of an app. They're the lifeblood of any Android game. The Bundle class is merely a method of saving the current status of the program.

Now, however, you look at the View class. Views handle the graphics and appearance of the screen while an application's running. All of your games will create a class that extends the View class and gives you this functionality. Often, you have significantly more code in your View class than in your Activity class because the majority of a game consists of manipulating objects on the screen.

All functional View classes must have two distinct parts. The first is a constructor method. Like any class, when you create an instance of it, you need to call a function that defines various aspects of the object. In the View class, you can load your images and determine the starting position for all your sprites.

The next critical part of the View class is a method that renders the images to the screen. This is called every time you move an image because the image must be redrawn in its new location.

Although this is an abstract way to see the class, it helps you get through the code. Before you dive in, however, let's look at the mechanics of actually taking a file and displaying it on the screen.

▪ **Tip** If you're curious about the View class or any other Android class, visit http://developer.android.com/reference/packages.html and find the package you're looking for. Here Android provides documentation on how to use the classes and the various methods that each class contains.

How Android Renders Images

The View class is only a part of the whole way that images are rendered to the screen. The other building blocks include an image, a way to store the image, a method to draw it, and the final result on the screen.

Images are stored in the project. The next section goes over how you add an image. Once the image is stored in the application, you access it by assigning it to a *bitmap*. A bitmap is your way of describing an image and get it ready for blitting to the screen.

Before it can be put on the display, it must be rendered through a *canvas*. A canvas holds the methods that draw the image. Inside a view, you call on the canvas to handle the drawing process. *Views* are designated sections of the screen that they control. In your case, the view owns the entire screen real estate. The canvas then draws the image to the screen.

Rendering an Image

To really understand how the View class works in Android, let's use it to display an image:

1. You need an image file to load onto the screen. You may have an image file ready to go, or you may need to create one. Any image on your computer that has a .png or .bmp extension is fine.

    a. If you have a ready-to-use image, make sure it's no more than 500×500 pixels.

    b.   If you want draw your own image, I usually use either Inkscape (http://inkscape.org/) or GIMP (www.gimp.org/) as my graphics editor because both are free to use. If you prefer your own graphics editor, that's fine as well.

2. Drag the file into the res drawable-mdpi folder of your GraphicsTest project. Eclipse asks if you want to copy it; click Yes, and you're ready to go.

3. If you look closely in the res folder of the project, you see it contains three folders that start with word drawable. These all specify a certain resolution of graphics on the device. For games that are built for the tablet, you use the medium definition folder; but if you were developing for phones, you would want to have a different version of each image at the three resolutions to ensure that most phones could render them as quickly as possible.

4. With the GameView.java file open in the editing pane, replace the code from Listing 2-1 with the code shown in Listing 2-2. This code renders your image to the tablet's screen. I explain what each piece does afterward.

Listing 2-2. GameView.java

```
package com.gameproject.graphicstest;

import android.content.Context;
import android.graphics.Bitmap;
import android.graphics.BitmapFactory;
import android.graphics.Canvas;
import android.graphics.Color;
import android.view.View;

class GameView extends View {
    public GameView(Context context) {
        super(context);
    }
```

```
    @Override
    public void onDraw(Canvas canvas) {
        Bitmap star = BitmapFactory.decodeResource(getResources(), R.drawable.star);
        canvas.drawColor(Color.BLACK);
        canvas.drawBitmap(star, 10, 10, null);
    }
}
```

5. Wow, things got complicated quickly. The code in Listing 2-2 is actually very straightforward, and you can probably understand most of it without much explanation.

6. The first major change is the addition of numerous new import statements. The majority of these invoke the graphics package from Android, whereas the last invokes the View class. The first import involves the Context class that you use as an argument for functions.

7. The start of the actual code shows how the class you created extends the functionality of the View class. This is a common practice in Java and simply inherits the methods and variables of the View class for your own use. If you didn't do this, you would be unable to draw images to the screen.

8. The first function, GameView, is a dummy function that doesn't initiate anything. You use it later, but right now, keep it there to satisfy Java's requirements of a class.

9. Finally, the meat of the source is the onDraw method that handles the changes to the screen. You use the @Override notation to run your version of the onDraw function rather than the original onDraw() provided by the View class. The argument to the method includes the very important Canvas that is responsible for the drawing of the image. The next line simply creates a new Bitmap object and uploads your image file into it. Because the image file I've used is named star.png, I've named its bitmap star. Substitute the name of your image in the three places that you see star written in this code. Alternatively, you can rename your image star.png and not have to change the code at all.

10. Next, you have the Canvas object color the entire screen black. This is redundant because black is the default, but it's good practice to keep this line. If you prefer a different background color, replace black with the name of your color. Note that Android accepts most traditional color names; but if you're looking for a specific shade of pink, you have to write out the RGB value, as shown in this statement:

```
canvas.drawColor(Color.argb(0, 100, 100, 100));
```

11. The argb function takes the amount of alpha, red, green, and blue color as arguments in the form of an integer.

12. The last line of the Listing 2-2 calls the drawBitmap method to draw the image to the screen. Notice that the arguments of this function are (Bitmap bitmap, float left, float top, Paint paint. You don't use the Paint object, so you pass a null value to it. You can change the location of the image by editing the values of the distance of the image from the top and left. After this, you want to see the fruits of your labor. Although you have a way to render an image to the

screen, your application will never use it because the start of the program doesn't call the drawing method. You change this by creating an instance of GameView in MainActivity. To do this, you must change a single line in the MainActivity.java file to point to your GameView class.

13. At the top of Eclipse, open the MainActivity.java file. Find the line that looks like this:

```
setContentView(R.layout.main);
```

14. You likely remember this as the line that tells the device to load the main.xml file as the layout of the app. You want to replace that XML with GameView.java. This is readily done by adding the statement in Listing 2-3 inside the MainActivity constructor.

Listing 2-3. Using GameView.java as the View

```
setContentView(new GameView(this));
```

15. The adition of this statement creates a new instance of the GameView class and loads it as the view of the application. You're now ready to try out your handiwork.

16. Click the green play button at the top of Eclipse, and the application starts. Follow the procedure from Chapter 1 when the simulator has begins to play the new app. If all goes well, your image, which began life as a .png file, is vibrantly displayed on the screen.

This result certainly isn't very exciting, so your next goal is to move the image on the screen.

Working with Sprites

Before you can move an image around the screen, you have to call it something. Games don't move images or shapes around but use *sprites* instead—objects whose presence on the screen is represented by an image but whose methods and properties provide the functionality and state you need to control and keep track of them. There are a number of advantages to creating a dedicated Sprite class. You can easily add animation sequences and rotation, and even keep track of the lives or ammo of each sprite. Before you create a Sprite class, let's work on a better way to display sprites and a more advanced game loop to handle their consistent movement and updating.

Rendering Sprites

You need to do some major revisions to the View class you created. First, let's use the SurfaceView class rather than the View class. This is a subtle distinction, but the SurfaceView class has advantages that speed up your rendering. You cover the ins and outs of the SurfaceView class when you look at animations in a later chapter. Listing 2-4 shows the new code for GameView.java. Change your current code to this new revision. It forms a base for your more advanced applications of images and sprites.

Listing 2-4. GameView.java

```java
package com.gameproject.graphicstest;

import android.content.Context;
import android.graphics.BitmapFactory;
import android.graphics.Canvas;
import android.graphics.Color;
import android.view.SurfaceHolder;
import android.view.SurfaceView;


public class GameView extends SurfaceView implements
                SurfaceHolder.Callback {

    public GameView(Context context) {
        super(context);

        setFocusable(true);

    }


    @Override
    public void surfaceChanged(SurfaceHolder holder, int format, int width, int height) {
        }

        @Override
        public void surfaceCreated(SurfaceHolder holder) {

        }

        @Override
        public void surfaceDestroyed(SurfaceHolder holder) {
        }


        public void onDraw(Canvas canvas) {
                canvas.drawColor(Color.BLACK);
        }

        public void update() {
        }


}
```

Right now, GameView.java doesn't perform any meaningful operations besides making the canvas black. You removed the drawing functions from the class so that you can implement them in your Sprite and Thread classes later. The first important piece of the new GameView class is that it now implements SurfaceHolder.Callback. This is responsible for controlling the surface and enabling you to draw on it from when it's created until it's destroyed. With this, you're given three methods you override: surfaceChanged, surfaceCreated, and surfaceDestroyed. You soon populate some of these with your instructions for dealing with sprites and the game loop.

You also use the constructor method of GameView when you need to initiate instances of your Sprite class. At the end of the code, you have onDraw and update functions. You used onDraw() to put your image on the screen earlier in the chapter, so it should look familiar. The update function is new; you use it to call each sprite to update itself. With an ability to handle the images, you can now explore how the game runs.

Building a Game Loop

To run the game well, you tap into the power of Java's Thread class. If you've done programming in a modern language, you've likely run into threads before. A *thread* is an independent routine that the device executes. Threads are nearly always used with other threads in what is called *multithreading*. This basically means that threads exist autonomously and are often run simultaneously by a program to perform different functions. An example is running the graphics of a game in one thread and handling the physics in another thread. Obviously these two things must happen at the same time, so you multithread the program.

To build Android games, you use the Java Thread class. You can find the source for the Thread class in Java.lang.Thread. You don't have to import this because it's assumed to be available; however, it's critical to remember that this is the class you're using. For your purposes, threads are very simple. You create a class that extends Thread, and then you override the run method and put your game loop there. From that place, you can change the view or deal with collisions or gather input.

Now that you see the changes that we have made in GameView, let's create the all important extension of the Thread class:

1. Make a new class in Eclipse, and name it GameLogic. Because GameView.java handles the appearance of your game, it's only appropriate that GameLogic.java handles the behind-the-scenes computations.

■ **Tip** As you make more and more source code files, it's a great help to name the classes very specifically. If you have a game that involves different types of sprites or objects, don't label the classes SpriteOne, SpriteTwo, and so on. I always attempt to name a class after its exact function, such as EnemySprite or FlyingSprite.

---

2. Listing 2-5 shows the entire listing for GameLogic.java. Similar to your implementation of the SurfaceView class, the current code is very spartan. Copy the code from Listing 2-5 to replace the original code of GameLogic.

Listing 2-5. GameLogic.java

```java
package com.gameproject.graphicstest;

import android.graphics.Canvas;
import android.view.SurfaceHolder;

public class GameLogic extends Thread {

    private SurfaceHolder surfaceHolder;
    private GameView mGameView;
    private int game_state;
    public static final int PAUSE = 0;
    public static final int READY = 1;
    public static final int RUNNING = 2;

    public GameLogic(SurfaceHolder surfaceHolder, GameView mGameView) {
        super();
        this.surfaceHolder = surfaceHolder;
        this.mGameView = mGameView;
    }


    public void setGameState(int gamestate) {
        this.game_state = gamestate;
    }
    public int getGameState(){
        return game_state;
    }

    @Override
    public void run() {

        Canvas canvas;
        while (game_state == RUNNING) {
                canvas = null;
                try {
                        canvas = this.surfaceHolder.lockCanvas();
                        synchronized (surfaceHolder) {
                                this.mGameView.update();
                                this.mGameView.onDraw(canvas);
                        }
                }
                finally {
                        if (canvas != null) {
                                surfaceHolder.unlockCanvasAndPost(canvas);
                        }
                }
        }
    }
}
```

Here is a list of the important methods of `GameLogic.java` and how each functions:

- **`SurfaceHolder()`**: Creates a means of manipulating the canvas. In the code for the `run()` function, it locks and unlocks the canvas that you draw on. *Locking* the canvas means that only this thread can write to it. You unlock it to allow any thread to work with it.

- **`Gameview()`**: Creates an instance of your `GameView` class and uses it to call the update and onDraw methods that you saw in the previous section.

- **`setGameState()`**: Creates a system for storing the state of the game at any given time. Later, you use this when you have a Pause screen or want to display a message when the player wins or loses the game. The game state also determines how long you perform the game loop.

- **`run()`**: When the game is in the running state, attempts to lock the canvas and then performs your necessary operations, releases the canvas, and prepares to start the process over again.

Although `GameLogic.java` may appear simple enough, it doesn't handle many of the issues that a game deals with. First, there is no timing system in place. The loop will run as fast as the processor will allow it to run, so a fast tablet will go quickly and a slower tablet will have a dramatically lower speed. Later, the chapter addresses this with a very simple way to regulate the amount that a sprite moves when you have a goal of around 30 frames per second (fps).

`GameLogic.java` also doesn't handle any tasks like input or collision detection that will be implemented later. For now, `GameLogic` is a tool to perform operations repeatedly without complicating the `GameView` class.

Creating a Sprite

The next step in building your game is to create the `Sprite` class. Although your game needs only one instance of `GameLogic` and `GameView`, you can have dozens of sprites in your game; so the code must be generic, yet allow you to perform all of your necessary operations on the sprites.

Because there is no real basis for a `Sprite` class in any Android package, you create the code from scratch. Basic variables are the root of your class. Examples are the x and y coordinates of the sprite as well as the sprite's image itself. You also want to store the sprite's speed in each direction. Eventually, the health and other aspects of your sprites will also be stored here. To keep the `Sprite` class pristine, you label all of these variables as `private` and use a function to change their values and retrieve their values. This is common practice and prevents you from inadvertently changing the values when you meant to retrieve them, or vice versa.

Listing 2-6 shows the code for your `SpriteObject` class. Go through the normal process of creating a new class in Eclipse, and then fill it with this code. The code does some very simple tasks, so you shouldn't have much trouble understanding it.

Listing 2-6. SpriteObject.java

```
package com.gameproject.graphicstest;

import android.graphics.Bitmap;
import android.graphics.Canvas;
```

```java
public class SpriteObject {

        private Bitmap bitmap;
        private int x;
        private int y;
        private int x_move = 5;
        private int y_move = 5;


        public SpriteObject(Bitmap bitmap, int x, int y) {
                this.bitmap = bitmap;
                this.x = x;
                this.y = y;
        }


        public int getX() {
                return x;
        }

        public int getY() {
                return y;
        }

        public Bitmap getBitmap() {
                return bitmap;
        }


        public void setX(int x) {
                this.x = x;
        }

        public void setY(int y) {
                this.y = y;
        }
        public void setBitmap(Bitmap bitmap) {
                this.bitmap = bitmap;
        }



        public void draw(Canvas canvas) {
            canvas.drawBitmap(bitmap, x - (bitmap.getWidth() / 2), y - (bitmap.getHeight() /
2), null);
        }


        public void update() {
```

```
                        x += (x_move);
                        y += (y_move);

        }

}
```

The last two methods of this class—draw() and update()—are the most intriguing. The draw function is called from the game loop in GameLogic.java. You use the update operation to increment the x and y coordinates before you render the image to the screen. Notice that you can change the speed of movement by altering the variables manually, or you can create functions that let you change the speed of the sprite based on an event like collisions or user input.

Running a Game

With some quick fixes to your GameView class, you can have a completed app that sends your sprite shooting down the screen. The first order of business is to create an instance of both the GameLogic and the SpriteObject class within GameView so you can tap into your newly created classes:

1. Open the GameView class so you can add some code to it.

2. Put the two instances of your classes (shown in Listing 2-7) before the GameView constructor.

Listing 2-7. Making Instances of Your Classes

```
private SpriteObject sprite;
private GameLogic mGameLogic;
```

3. Inside the GameView class, you call the constructor of both classes. Be extra careful about how the arguments are structured, however. The final line gives you the ability to work with the device. Add the code in Listing 2-8 inside the GameView constructor.

Listing 2-8. Constructing the New Classes

```
sprite = new SpriteObject(BitmapFactory.decodeResource(getResources(), R.drawable.star), 50,
50);
mGameLogic = new GameLogic(getHolder(), this);
getHolder().addCallback(this);
```

4. SpriteObject takes a bitmap and the coordinates of the sprite. The way to get the bitmap resource is identical to what you did in the first example in this chapter. GameLogic takes a SurfaceHolder and a GameView. The function getHolder() is part of the SurfaceView class that lets you send the current holder to the method.

5. Now you get to take advantage of the new objects in the surfaceCreated function. Listing 2-9 shows the code you use to start the game loop as soon as the application creates the surface.

Listing 2-9. Starting the Game Loop

```
@Override
public void surfaceCreated(SurfaceHolder holder) {
        mGameLogic.setGameState(GameLogic.RUNNING);
        mGameLogic.start();
}
```

6. With the meat of your game started, you have to put your methods into the onDraw and update routines, as shown in Listing 2-10. Notice that the GameView class has no call to these functions; they're instead called from the GameLogic class.

Listing 2-10. Using the Objects in the Game

```
public void onDraw(Canvas canvas) {
        canvas.drawColor(Color.BLACK);
        sprite.draw(canvas);
}

public void update() {
        sprite.update();
}
```

7. The onDraw method gets the sprite to draw itself, and then the update function has the sprite perform its own update function. Separating the update methods from GameView reduces the clutter inside the class. Whenever a specific task must be performed, do it in a separate function to keep your main code clean.

8. All of your code is in place, and the game can now be executed. Make sure all of the Java sources are saved, and then start the simulator by clicking the green Eclipse play button.

▪ **Note** If you receive errors about not being able to find a class, you may have created your Java files in a different folder. In the file tree in the left pane, make sure all four files are in the src folder.

If all goes well, you should see the image quickly crossing the screen from upper left to lower right. As you noticed before, depending on the computer or device that is running the program, the sprite may move quickly or slowly. With the ability to control the movement of your sprite, you can change the x_move and y_move values to speed it up or slow it down. The next section deals with cleaning up the user interface and getting ready for some intense games.

Getting a Professional Look

Games are meant to be played as immersively as possible. To make this possible on a tablet or any device, you have to remove all the bars and menus that remind the player of the world outside their game. Android has some features that make this effective, but Android 3.0 includes features that actually mandate having the system bar always visible. Regardless, you can hide the action bar with a simple line in the MainActivity.java file. Listing 2-11 shows the statement that should go right after the super command.

Listing 2-11. *Removing the Action Bar*

```
getActionBar().hide();
```

If you run the project now, the top bar that has the Android robot icon in it is gone. The image should move across the screen as normal. To make your game look more professional, you can change the default icon into something more suitable for your game. When a player wants to open your game, they go to their homepage and select the app. Providing a vibrant icon that grabs their attention is important.

Before creating your own icon, jot down the icon sizes. You need to have 72×72, 48×48, and 32×32 versions. In your graphics editor, create an icon with the largest dimensions, and then scale it down for the others. When you have the three files, name them icon.png and replace the other icon files in each of the resolution categories under the res folder.

For now, the only other work to be done is to put a header on your code, like the one shown in Listing 2-12, so you can distribute your game without worrying about people taking your work without giving you credit. Granted, anything posted online is liable to be used inappropriately, but putting your signature on your work can help people ask you questions or at least give credit where credit is due.

Listing 2-12. *A Sample Comment Header Above Your Code*

```
/******************************************************************
 * GraphicsTest - illustration of basic sprite principles       *
 *                                                               *
 * Author:  Kerfs, Jeremy                                        *
 *                                                               *
 * Last Modified: Jan 1st, 2000                                  *
 *                                                               *
 * Version: 1.0                                                  *
 *                                                               *
 ******************************************************************/
```

If you're really interested in protecting your work, you can release the code under a license. For example, the Android code itself is released under the Apache License Version 2.0, which is very liberal in allowing users to use the code largely for whatever projects they can dream up. If you release your code online, be ready to offer it under a license that keeps it open source and lets others develop on it.

■ **Tip** For more information about the Creative Commons license and how open source projects work, go to http://creativecommons.org/.

Implementing Timing and Complex Motion

Now you can move on to create a system that enables you to accurately set how quickly your game runs. No longer will the game loop be subject to the whims of the device. To do this, you use a timer and then adjust the movement based on how much time has elapsed. This means that if one cycle takes a very long time and another takes a short amount of time, the sprite will move a certain distance depending on that value. Looking at the code is the best way to understand this type of method. Follow these steps:

1. Replace the code in the synchronized block in GameLogic.java with the code in Listing 2-13.

Listing 2-13. Testing a Constant FPS Game

```
try {
Thread.sleep(30);
}
catch (InterruptedException e1) {
}

long time_interim = System.currentTimeMillis();
int adj_mov = (int)(time_interim - time_orig);

mGameView.update(adj_mov);
time_orig = time_interim;
this.mGameView.onDraw(canvas);
```

2. At first, this entire snippet looks foreign. In reality, it performs a couple of simple tasks:

   • The try-catch block tells the tablet to wait for 30 milliseconds before continuing. This operation can produce an exception that you don't deal with.

   • Previously, in the run function right next to the declaration of the Canvas object, you made two long variables named time_orig and time_interim. Time_orig was set to the current system time with long time_orig = System.currentTimeMillis();. Now you set time_interim to the time and determine how much time has elapsed. You store this in the integer adj_mov, which stands for *adjusted movement*. The Update function in the GameView class is changed to accept this integer as an argument. When this has been completed, the original time is set to the current time, and the view is refreshed by calling the onDraw method.

3. Add the code from Listing 2-14 to the update method in GameView.

Listing 2-14. GameView.java with Revised update Function

```
public void update(int adj_mov) {
      sprite.update(adj_mov);
   }
```

4. Listing 2-15 shows that the adj_mov variable is passed along to the sprite in order for it to be incorporated into the movement.

Listing 2-15. SpriteObject.java with Revised update Function

```
public void update(int adj_mov) {
```

```
        x += (adj_mov * x_move);
        y += (adj_mov * y_move);
}
```

5. In this case, the sprite update method multiplies x_move and y_move by the change in time. I changed the speed constants to 1 in order to keep the movement at a reasonable pace. This makes sense because if the computations take a long time, then the movement is multiplied by a greater number. If the processing is quick, the sprite doesn't move nearly as far. The idea of controlling a game's frames per second has a variety of implications that you take advantage of in later projects.

Although you would imagine most games wanting to have a time element, many apps can get away without worrying about this. Think about a chess or tic-tac-toe game. In a turn-based game, timing isn't an important aspect.

■ **Note** Sample programs are available from Android's reference guide that you can look to for inspiration on different types of games. Check out this page for the code sources: `http://developer.android.com/resources/browser.html?tag=sample`. Be wary of the fact that the majority of the programs were written for earlier versions of Android, such as 2.2 or 2.3. You may want to create an emulator specific to that version if you're truly interested in the examples. Porting them to Android 3.0 isn't difficult; you can probably do so by enlarging the graphics and screen size.

Detecting Collisions

Although you haven't worked with gathering input from the user, you can instill a certain amount of responsiveness in the game by dealing with simple collisions with the walls of the tablet. A quick and simple implementation is shown in Listing 2-16.

Listing 2-16. Collision Code

```
if (sprite.getX() >= getWidth()){
        sprite.setMoveX(-2);
}
if (sprite.getX() <= 0){
        sprite.setMoveX(2);
}
```

Add this excerpt into the update method of the GameView.java file. It's important to do this before the call to sprite.update() because you must handle any direction changes before you increment the position of the sprite.

You may notice that you reference a function that you haven't yet created. To make this function work, the SpriteObject class needs two functions called setMoveX and setMoveY. The basic code for these is shown in Listing 2-17.

Listing 2-17. Collision Functions

```
public void setMoveX(int movex){
        x_move = movex;
}
public void setMoveY(int movey){
        y_move = movey;
}
```

Before you run this program, I manually changed the y_move to zero so that you can eliminate any up and down movement. When you play the program, the sprite should bounce back and forth between the right and left sides of the screen. There should be something strange about the movement, though: when the sprite gets to the far right onscreen, it disappears most of the way because you're referencing your collisions on the location of the sprite, which is given by its center. You can eliminate any disappearance by taking into account the actual size and dimensions of the sprite.

If you wish to experiment with the necessary changes, go ahead and manipulate the if statement to reflect the sprite's absolute left as well as its absolute right. Chapter 7 goes in depth in a discussion of collisions; you use the RECT element to precisely find intersections between different sprites and the walls or floor.

░ **Note** Collision detection is a critical aspect of almost any game, and there are a variety of ways to go about it. When you later want to use bullets or other irregular shapes, you can employ a variety of polygons to find the intersection of sprites. A quick search on *irregular collision detection* yields a wealth of information to continue this topic.

Summary

This chapter covered the methods of rendering images, and you made a framework to manage sprites and move them around the screen at a consistent rate. With this work, most games should be doable with your current system. In the next couple of chapters, adding user input and sounds will make a quality game possible. You work on advanced graphics topics later, when you use OpenGL to speed up graphics for complex games and add an animation framework to your Sprite class. All this code is written with the goal of being reusable and applicable to any number of games.

To cap off this chapter, make sure all the code and examples run properly on your system. If you made any mistakes, you can download the code for Chapter 2 from the website associated with this book. Before moving on, you need to understand this information so you can easily tackle artificial intelligence and advanced physics, which expand on the ideas of consistent motion according to a time schedule.

The next chapter covers a totally different topic: user input. Your sprites can come to come to life and respond to what the user does. This is a very exciting portion of game development because it's the core of interactivity. Otherwise you'd be designing a complicated movie.

CHAPTER 3

Gathering User Input

So far, your work has lacked the interactivity of a game, chiefly because you have no means of letting players interact with the sprites and characters. In this chapter, you unlock several forms of input that you eventually use to control the look and actions that take place in the game. This is also where you get to unlock some of the amazing features of tablet game programming in Android 3.0. Previously, most of such work was applicable to older Android phones, but now programmers heavily rely on large touchscreens to gather touch input.

Unique to the tablet, the user can make large selections; and as a developer, you need to prepare for this. In addition to this obvious method of interaction, you look at some more unusual inputs, such as accelerometer data and gestures. Along with input, you cover how event queues can help streamline your games. But let's begin with a quick overview of the input devices found on most Android tablets.

Understanding Tablet Input Options

To understand your options, you need to know what tablets offer in terms of gathering data about the user's actions. Following is a fairly comprehensive list of the sensors that exist in many tablets. Some tablets don't have all of these, whereas others have additional ones:

- *Touchscreen:* Most tablets have a multitouch interface that lets you use input from several fingers on the screen at one time. The accurate screens now let you create very small sprites and still enable the user to drag them around due to the screens' precision. For the majority of games, this is the method of user control. Nearly every game needs this for its menus at the very least.

- *Microphone:* Tablets running Android 3.0 often have a built-in microphone that can be used as input. Examples include altering the height of a helicopter based on either the pitch or the volume of the sound sampling. Although this has many interesting applications, it isn't used in most games.

- *Accelerometer:* This sensor measures changes in orientation of a tablet. You may be familiar with this when you rotate your tablet from landscape to portrait view: the screen generally adjusts itself based on data from an accelerometer. In flight games and racing games, this is a fun way to let the user control their vehicle.

- *Gyroscope:* Similar to the accelerometer, a gyroscope measures the rate of turns along the three axis of movement. This is used for precise motion and can tell you the exact patterns of rotation. Games that use the accelerometer can also use a gyroscope.

- *Proximity:* A proximity sensor measures an object's distance from the phone. Often these are imprecise and are used primarily to turn off a screen if it's close to your cheek (when you're making a call with a touchscreen phone). Very few games use this, however.

Although this list includes most of the ways for a game to gather data from the player, you can access other sensors that describe the player's area and surroundings. This is no substitute for user interaction, but it adds realism to a game. Following are the ways most tablets provide to get this information:

- *GPS:* The GPS location of a device can let the game map be an image of the surrounding area or can change the scenery or characters of a game. It's impossible to take into account all the various locations that a device can be in, but later you examine ways to incorporate this.

- *Ambient light:* This sensor is primarily used to adjust the brightness of the screen depending on the external light, but it does offer some advantages to game developers. One way to incorporate it is to change the game to a night scene if the user is in a dark place.

- *Barometer:* This sensor is more of a joke than anything. But in reality, a game could potentially use it to approximate the altitude and adjust the game accordingly. I haven't yet seen a game integrate this sensor successfully.

Knowing the various internal sensors you can expect to find on a tablet, you can also begin to think about additional input devices you might want to connect to it. Android 3.0 comes with the best support for Bluetooth input of any Android version. Each new release will likely continue to expand this. Although Bluetooth input may be exciting, the point of writing games for a tablet is to provide users with a unique experience. If they still must connect their game console, then they may as well use a television. With that being said, Android now has native support for joysticks, keyboards, and game controllers.

▪ **Note** With the advent of televisions that run a hybrid of the Android and Chrome operating systems, it's becoming possible to use a tablet as a controller. Connecting a tablet to a TV that runs Android allows the television screen to display the game while the tablet doubles as a map and controller. The more widely Android is used to power devices, the more opportunities you have in terms of input.

You're almost ready to get your hands dirty setting up some input for your games. First, however, you go over some of the theory behind gathering input. Getting input quickly is critical to a game, whereas a traditional application (a map or an address book, for example) doesn't require this speed.

Understanding Tablet Input

For a traditional application, the program usually depends on an input event. What this means is that nothing happens until the user interacts with the app. Most apps have many different menus and text, and the code is responsible for sifting through it as soon as the user presses a button. In these cases, a traditional game loop isn't necessary because there is nothing to do until a touch event happens. The same principle applies to older programs for phones that didn't have touchscreens.

If you wish to make this sort of app, Android makes it very simple for you to add listeners to the various buttons and images on the screen. By performing specific actions when a button is pressed, you can manipulate the program's screen and actions. Surprisingly, this way of working with a tablet has some relevance for games. Take for example a turn-based strategy game (such as chess): nothing occurs until the player moves a sprite.

All methods of gathering user input inevitably involve the very important *game process*. This is the cycle of events the app goes through. There are nearly as many types of game processes as there are genres of games. These cycles all process input, determine physics, and give the user feedback (usually by changing the game's display). Figure 3-1 shows the game process used for a turn-based strategy game.

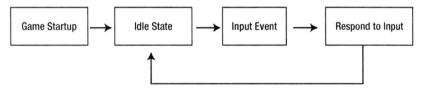

Figure 3-1. The game process for an input-dependent game

■ **Note** If you're interested in turn-based games, you can check out several examples online. A very simple but elegant demonstration is the Android sample of a tic-tac-toe game. You can download the source here: http://developer.android.com/resources/samples/TicTacToeMain/index.html.

Because the majority of modern games are fast-paced and input-intensive, you work on handling input events while you're also performing graphics and logic operations. To do this, you gather input and process it, so as to not interrupt the flow of the game. You may think of this as simultaneously doing separate things at the same time; but more realistically, you're noting an input event and then waiting to handle it when you reach the next game cycle. Figure 3-2 shows how input events are stored until you're ready to handle them.

The Thread class discussed in Chapter 2 plays a large role in handling input events. However, the View class is the place for methods that register an input event. In fact, the View class has several methods that you override to perform your own work on touch events.

You materially alter your Sprite class because you already have methods like setX(int) and setY(int) that let you manipulate the sprite once an input event has occurred. You create new events that change the speed and direction of sprites. Later, a touch event can potentially cause the sprite to reload its ammo or cast a special spell. By the end of this chapter, you'll be using certain events to spawn the creation of a brand-new sprite.

To get a clear idea of how the example game works, Figure 3-2 illustrates how you handle input events without stalling the game if the user starts quickly tapping the screen. Be careful to notice the differences between Figure 3-1 and Figure 3-2.

The version of the game process that you use has two additions that aren't present in the turn-based game illustrated in Figure 3-1. First, the application path isn't linear: input events are added to the game as they're needed. Second, the game loop manages the entire process, whereas the processing loop in a turn-based game is controlled by the input. This is a critical difference because your games need to proceed regardless of what the user is doing, whereas the game in Figure 3-1 must wait for a user interaction.

Your game's graphics rendering is also different in that it happens constantly. In a turn-based game, the graphics are changed after a user-input event occurs. But you'll update the graphics in each cycle of the loop even if nothing has changed.

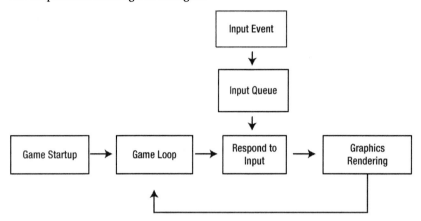

Figure 3-2. *The game loop for a continuous game*

Figure 3-2 shows a continuous game process that loops through graphics and user input. Any game cycle that continues without necessitating user input can be referred to as a *game loop*. Notice that an input event leads to an input queue where the event is stored until you're ready to accept and respond to it. Because your game runs at a high number of frames per second, you don't have any noticeable lag in input responsiveness.

Responding to Touch

Android works on a variety of devices, so it has methods to gather all types of input. For you, however, the most important events are interactions with the touchscreen. Your number-one method is the following:

```
Public boolean onTouchEvent(MotionEvent event){
}
```

This method is inherited from the View class, and you override it in order to perform your own operations. The key aspect of this function is the parameter it contains. A MotionEvent is an object in Android that describes a variety of interactions with the tablet. You can find out a lot about the event by calling methods in the MotionEvent class. This class has many options, but the important functions are pointed out as you use them. If you're curious, you can look up the class in the Android documentation: http://developer.android.com/reference/android/view/MotionEvent.html.

Again, this and several other methods are called from within your GameView class, so you can quickly pass relevant changes to your Sprite and GameLogic processes. Other input functions that you may deal with include onKeyDown(), onClick(), and onKeyUp(). If you're interested in using these, they can be implemented nearly identically to how you handle generic touch events. Each of these methods returns a boolean value. This means that when you're finished processing, you return **true**, to free the program to gather the next input.

As you can imagine, with a tablet, a single swipe of the screen may seem relatively simple to a player; but your app may misinterpret it as several small movements or miss the movement entirely. As you go, you work on more complex gestures and make sure that even a new player can grasp your game's controls.

Let's take a closer look at how you can handle user input from a touchscreen. Create anew project in Eclipse to demonstrate user input:

1. Choose File ↗ New ↗ Project ↗ Android Project. Type the name of the new project as **InputTest**, and make sure the Activity is entitled **MainActivity**. It's common practice to put your projects in the same root package.

2. Because you're largely going to reuse classes from earlier, open the folder tree of GraphicsTest and copy all four `.java` files to the `src` folder of the InputTest project. Also close the window of each class in your editing pane, to make sure you're editing the new project's files. Open all the classes for the InputTest project, and you're almost ready to get started.

3. If you still want the same image, move the image file from `res` ↗ `drawable_mdpi` to the new project's folder. If you desire, you can create a new image to go with this project, as long as you refer to it properly in the code.

4. You already know that input gathering occurs in the `GameView` class, so add the function in Listing 3-1 to GameView. Put this section right beneath the `surfacedestroyed()` method.

▓ **Note** Many of the topics discussed require additional `import` statements at the top of your code. The heading for each listing includes the necessary `import` statements. Make sure you place these at the top of your file, or you won't be able to run the app.

Listing 3-1. Adding Input Gathering to GameView.java *(import* android.view.MotionEvent*)*

```
@Override
public boolean onTouchEvent(MotionEvent event){
        return true;
}
```

5. This is the full implementation of onTouchEvent; however, it currently doesn't perform any meaningful operation. Add the snippet shown in Listing 3-2 to the code of the function before the **return** statement.

Listing 3-2. Manipulating the Sprite Based on a Touch Event

```
sprite.setX((int)event.getX());
sprite.setY((int)event.getY());
```

6. This code uses your setX and setY functions to move the sprite to wherever the touch event stopped or to the last position of the finger. Event.getX is a way to retrieve the location of the last movement event. It returns a float, so you cast it into an integer to satisfy your method.

7. Because your sprite is constantly zipping across the screen, you remove the sprite's movement. Listing 3-3 stops the changed `update()` method in the `GameView` class.

Listing 3-3. Stopping the Sprite Movement

```
public void update(int adj_mov) {
        if (sprite.getX()  > = getWidth()){
                sprite.setMoveX(0);
        }
        if (sprite.getX() <= 0){
                sprite.setMoveX(0);
        }
        sprite.update(adj_mov);

}
```

8. You must also stop the movement in the `SpriteObject` class by putting a zero as the value for the sprite-movement variables.

9. Your background work is complete. Save all the files, and run the app. If you click the screen, the sprite appears at the location of your last movement.

Also try dragging your cursor over the tablet. You see the sprite frenetically trying to keep up, even though it lags significantly if you're using a simulator. A real device has fairly fluid motion. Figure 3-3 shows the result of your work.

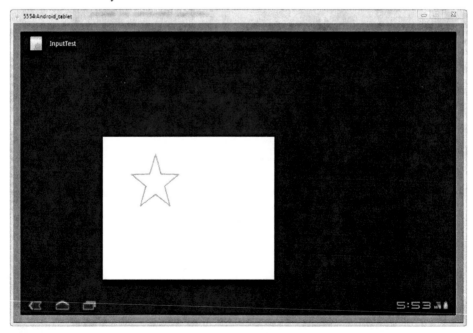

Figure 3-3. The star.png sprite was moved to a different location by dragging across the screen.

When you move your cursor on the screen, you may notice that the sprite moves regardless of where you start your movement. Most games that let you move a sprite have several sprites, so you must select which sprite you wish to move by touching it first. This brings you to one of the major topics of touchscreen input: *gestures*. Even though a drag event is inherently simple, it's considered a gesture because it involves a sustained interaction. Other gestures include scrolling, pinching, rotating, and so on. You learn next how you can create gestures and respond to them within the context of your games.

Responding to Gestures

To do all this magic, you need to become very friendly with the `Gesture` class in the Android SDK. Before you work with it in your code, let's play around with gestures in a sample program created by the Android development team. You can access this app within the simulator: it's called GestureBuilder. Before you do that, though, you have to make some changes to the simulator:

1. GestureBuilder writes files to a tablet's SD card. If your simulator doesn't have this, you can add it easily. Choose Window ↗ Android SDK and AVD Manager.

2. Click the tablet device, and click the Edit button at left on the screen. A dialog box pops up (as shown in Figure 3-4) in which you type an amount of memory for the device. I usually use 1,000 megabytes.

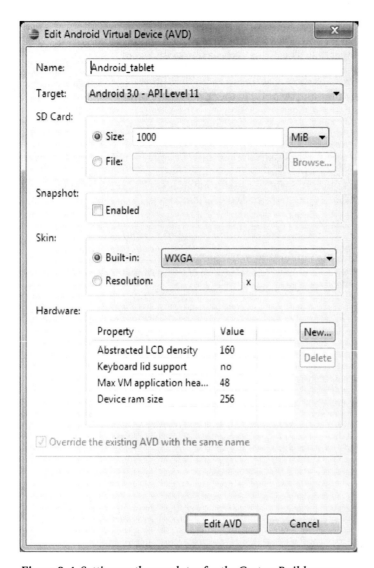

Figure 3-4. Setting up the emulator for the GestureBuilder app

3. Click Edit AVD.

4. You're brought back to the Android SDK and AVD Manager. Click the Start button; or, if the Start button isn't available, first select the emulator name, as shown in Figure 3-5. You're initiating the emulator from here because you want to be able to select the app rather than have an app start by default.

Figure 3-5. Launching the emulator from the Android SDK and AVD Manager

5. When the emulator is up and running, go to the icon labeled Apps. Then, click the GestureBuilder program.

6. Play around with this app for a bit to see how it works. Make a new gesture, and give it a name. Do a series of swipes to create your gesture. This application gives you a feel for what a gesture looks like.

If you created a truly great gesture that you want to use in a game, you can get the gesture from the SD card and reference it in your game code. This is an advanced topic, and you just want to experience gestures for now; to do this process, following the instructions in the Android documentation: http://developer.android.com/resources/articles/gestures.html.

Figure 3-6 shows a star gesture that I created. Even though you can draw a star in many ways, gestures are specific in that the *order* of the strokes is critical. The tablet is looking for the correct sequence.

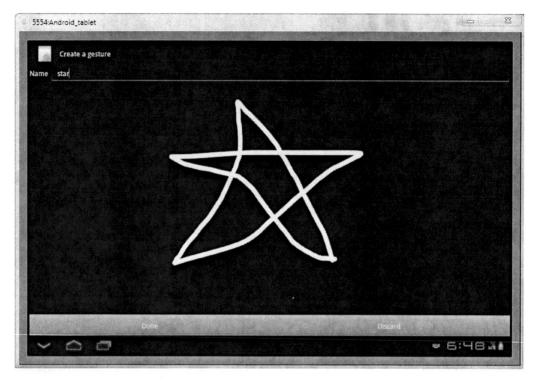

Figure 3-6. Making a unique star gesture

The Android development group has its own program called GestureDemo that lets you perform gestures for the app to recognize. This chapter doesn't go over the ins and outs of how the app works because it has limited relevance to most games. However, it's worth looking at briefly because you can see how gestures are recognized. By changing your way of performing a gesture, you find out how accurate the tablet is at recognizing it:

7. Download the project from http://code.google.com/p/apps-for-android/downloads/detail?name=GesturesDemos.zip&can=2&q=. Unzip the folder, and be careful to remember where everything was extracted.

8. Open Eclipse, and choose File ↗ Import ↗ General ↗ Existing Projects into Workspace.

9. Locate the folder GestureDemo that you downloaded, and fill out the form. When you click Finish, you have a new project in your workspace. To learn more about this project, you can visit the web page http://developer.android.com/resources/articles/gestures.html.

10. Run the new project, and begin performing gestures. If you do a lightning-bolt-type gesture, it should display Thunder Spell at the bottom.

If you play around with the project long enough, you may notice that it isn't very accurate at recognizing some gestures. This is to be expected and is one reason it's unusual to create custom gestures. The notable gestures that people are already familiar with, such as pinch and drag, are easily computed by Android and result in much less confusion. Nonetheless, some games are very exciting when you can use your hands to perform actions just as you would in real life. You can look up the Gestures library in the Android documentation to understand gestures better because it is too complicated of a topic to completely cover in this chapter.

■ **Tip** If you create your own gestures, make them simple and exaggerated. Also, limit your game to one or two new gestures that are very, very different from each other, to avoid mistakes.

Using Input Queues

Earlier, the chapter discussed how massive amounts of user input can freeze a game and cause it to stall. You can address this possibility with the very handy `InputObject` class. Basically, you're trying to limit the strain that is put on your main thread when input events happen. Recall that Figure 3-2 showed how you hold input events before responding to them. This is exactly what you do here. Instead of waiting to lock up the entire thread, you do the majority of the work in the background.

This system was originally introduced to me by Robert Green, and it's so efficient and simple that I have used it ever since. (You can read Robert's blog about Android development and other musings at www.rbgrn.net/.) An `ArrayBlockingQueue` does the heavy lifting for input handling. This is basically a method for storing objects and then iterating through them later. To use an `ArrayBlockingQueue`, you need to import it at the top of each Java file that uses it, as follows:

```
import java.util.concurrent.ArrayBlockingQueue;
```

To use this convenient method of storing input events and then handling them later, create a new class in your InputTest project called `InputObject`. From now on, you reference `InputObjects` rather than `MotionEvents` to get information about what type of event occurred. There are a variety of reasons for creating a class like this in addition to speeding up the processing. When you start responding to input, you'll notice the increased ease of working with sometimes complex events.

Let's try this technique:

1. Create the `InputObject` class, and populate it with the code in Listing 3-4.

Listing 3-4. InputObject.java

```
import java.util.concurrent.ArrayBlockingQueue;
import android.view.KeyEvent;
import android.view.MotionEvent;

public class InputObject {
        public static final byte EVENT_TYPE_KEY = 1;
        public static final byte EVENT_TYPE_TOUCH = 2;
        public static final int ACTION_KEY_DOWN = 1;
        public static final int ACTION_KEY_UP = 2;
        public static final int ACTION_TOUCH_DOWN = 3;
        public static final int ACTION_TOUCH_MOVE = 4;
        public static final int ACTION_TOUCH_UP = 5;
```

```
public ArrayBlockingQueue<InputObject> pool;
public byte eventType;
public long time;
public int action;
public int keyCode;
public int x;
public int y;

public InputObject(ArrayBlockingQueue<InputObject> pool) {
        this.pool = pool;
}

public void useEvent(KeyEvent event) {
        eventType = EVENT_TYPE_KEY;
        int a = event.getAction();
        switch (a) {
        case KeyEvent.ACTION_DOWN:
                action = ACTION_KEY_DOWN;
                break;
        case KeyEvent.ACTION_UP:
                action = ACTION_KEY_UP;
                break;
        default:
                action = 0;
        }
        time = event.getEventTime();
        keyCode = event.getKeyCode();
}

public void useEvent(MotionEvent event) {
        eventType = EVENT_TYPE_TOUCH;
        int a = event.getAction();
        switch (a) {
        case MotionEvent.ACTION_DOWN:
                action = ACTION_TOUCH_DOWN;
        break;
        case MotionEvent.ACTION_MOVE:
                action = ACTION_TOUCH_MOVE;
                break;
        case MotionEvent.ACTION_UP:
                action = ACTION_TOUCH_UP;
                break;
        default:
                action = 0;
        }
        time = event.getEventTime();
        x = (int) event.getX();
        y = (int) event.getY();
}

public void useEventHistory(MotionEvent event, int historyItem) {
        eventType = EVENT_TYPE_TOUCH;
```

```
            action = ACTION_TOUCH_MOVE;
            time = event.getHistoricalEventTime(historyItem);
            x = (int) event.getHistoricalX(historyItem);
            y = (int) event.getHistoricalY(historyItem);
    }

    public void returnToPool() {
            pool.add(this);
    }
}
```

2. Let's dissect this class. Input events like a `KeyEvent` or `MotionEvent` are processed by the function `useEvent()` in order to create the object that has the type of the action as well as relevant data about it, like the x and y coordinates of a touchscreen event. The key part to understand is how the `ArrayBlockingQueue` works.

3. It makes more sense in the context of integration into your other classes; but for now, let it suffice that `InputObjects` are stored in reverse order of their addition to the pool of events. This means the first event to occur is processed first. Obviously, user input must be handled in the order in which it happens.

4. Of special note in the listing is `useEventHistory()`. Methods like `getHistoricalEventTime()` and `getHistoricalX()` are used to get the original data of a motion event. Often, a swipe on the screen has several coordinates and times associated with it, so this is your means of getting the original location of the event versus the current cursor position.

5. Before moving on, also note that each event has a variable called `action` that stores the type of event that occurred. When you want to respond to the input, you can look up what type of event it was and respond accordingly. This saves you from performing a lot of guesswork.

6. To implement your new `InputObject` class, you need to make some major changes to `GameView.java`. Inside the `GameView` class, create the following variable shown in Listing 3-5.

Listing 3-5. Adding an inputObjectPool Object

```
private ArrayBlockingQueue<InputObject> inputObjectPool;
```

7. Under the `GameView(Context context)`, add the line in Listing 3-6.

Listing 3-6. Creating the InputObject Pool

```
createInputObjectPool();
```

8. You build this function in the `GameView` class with the code shown in Listing 3-7, which you place at the end of `GameView`.

Listing 3-7. Declaring a Function for Making the Object Pool

```
private void createInputObjectPool() {
```

```
        inputObjectPool = new ArrayBlockingQueue<InputObject>(20);
        for (int i = 0; i < 20; i++) {
                inputObjectPool.add(new InputObject(inputObjectPool));
        }
}
```

9. Here you initialize the `inputObjectPool` that stores your input objects. You make it 20 units long because you'll likely never exceed this limit (input events can only happen so fast). The `for` loop populates the pool with all the elements.

10. To start sending information to the input object pool, you need to modify the `onTouchEvent` that you worked with before. Type the code from Listing 3-8 into the `onTouchEvent()` method.

Listing 3-8. onTouchEvent(MotionEvent event)

```
@Override
public boolean onTouchEvent(MotionEvent event) {
        try {
                int hist = event.getHistorySize();
                if (hist > 0) {
                        for (int i = 0; i < hist; i++) {
                                InputObject input = inputObjectPool.take();
                                input.useEventHistory(event, i);
                                mGameLogic.feedInput(input);
                        }
                }
                InputObject input = inputObjectPool.take();
                input.useEvent(event);
                mGameLogic.feedInput(input);
        } catch (InterruptedException e) {
        }
        try {
                Thread.sleep(16);
        } catch (InterruptedException e) {
        }
        return true;
}
```

11. Notice that you lose the functionality of moving the sprite depending on the positon of the touch event. You add this piece back in the next section. In the onTouchEvent, you work with a **try** block to attempt to resolve each event into an InputObject and then store it for later processing. The call to mGameLogic.feedInput(input) is where you further access the event when the thread has the opportunity. Finally, you cause the main thread to sleep for 16 milliseconds to make sure you don't gather too much input at one time.

12. Reference the calls of useEvent and useEventHistory to their declarations in the InputObject class. You should be able to see how you create this listing of the input events that have occurred.

13. You need to add two new methods to the GameView class in GameView.java; see Listing 3-9. They're called by the GameLogic to work with the input objects. You disregard KeyEvent for now because tablets don't often worry about keyboard input. MotionEvent, however, is handled just as you did earlier by instructing the sprite to move to wherever the user last touched.

Listing 3-9. Processing Motion and Key Events

```
public void processMotionEvent(InputObject input){
        sprite.setX(input.x);
        sprite.setY(input.y);
}
public void processKeyEvent(InputObject input){

}
```

14. To set the sprite's x and y position, you access the input object's last coordinates. This simple process lets you visualize your operations better when you've abstracted the MotionEvent.

15. To finish your new input pipeline method, you add some code to the GameLogic class. Listing 3-10 declares two objects that you need to create. Place this code right beneath the variables that store the game state, such as PAUSE, READY, and RUNNING.

Listing 3-10. Declaring New Objects for Input Methods

```
private ArrayBlockingQueue<InputObject> inputQueue = new ArrayBlockingQueue<InputObject>(20);
private Object inputQueueMutex = new Object();
```

16. You need to make only one change to the run() method, but it's important that you place it in the correct location. Listing 3-11 shows the entire run() function with the addition highlighted.

Listing 3-11. Telling the Main Thread to Process the Input

```
@Override
public void run() {
        long time_orig = System.currentTimeMillis();
        long time_interim;
        Canvas canvas;

        while (game_state == RUNNING) {
                canvas = null;
                try {

                        canvas = this.surfaceHolder.lockCanvas();

                        synchronized (surfaceHolder) {
                try {
                    Thread.sleep(30);
```

```
                            } catch (InterruptedException e1) {
                            }
                            time_interim = System.currentTimeMillis();
                            int adj_mov = (int)(time_interim - time_orig);
                            mGameView.update(adj_mov);
                            processInput();  //this is the new way to process input.
                            time_orig = time_interim;
                            this.mGameView.onDraw(canvas);
                            }
                            }
                            finally {
                                    if (canvas != null) {
                                            surfaceHolder.unlockCanvasAndPost(canvas);
                                    }
                            }
            }
}
}
```

17. You must now define two functions because you've already created methods
     that call them. ProcessInput() is where the thread issues instructions about
     dealing with the input. Feedinput() handles the operation of the
     ArrayBlockingQueue. Place these methods, whose code appears in Listing 3-12,
     right below the run() function.

Listing 3-12. Feeding and Processing Input

```java
public void feedInput(InputObject input) {
        synchronized(inputQueueMutex) {
                try {
                        inputQueue.put(input);
                } catch (InterruptedException e) {
                }
        }
}

private void processInput() {
        synchronized(inputQueueMutex) {
                ArrayBlockingQueue<InputObject> inputQueue = this.inputQueue;
                while (!inputQueue.isEmpty()) {
                        try {
                                InputObject input = inputQueue.take();
                                if (input.eventType == InputObject.EVENT_TYPE_KEY) {
                                        mGameView.processKeyEvent(input);
                                } else if (input.eventType == InputObject.EVENT_TYPE_TOUCH) {
                                        mGameView.processMotionEvent(input);
                                }
                                input.returnToPool();
                        } catch (InterruptedException e) {
                        }
                }
        }
}
```

FeedInput() is very straightforward. It grabs the thread with synchronized() and has the input incorporated into the inputQueue. This method is called by the GameView class once the input object has satisfactorily categorized.

ProcessInput() is somewhat more complex in how it deals with the inputQueue. It also uses synchronized() to hold the thread, while it goes through the objects in the inputQueue and either has processKeyEvent() or processMotionEvent() take care of them. Both of those functions are defined in GameView.java because you want to be able to issue instructions to your sprite objects there.

After that magnificent change in code, your program now does exactly what it did in the beginning of the chapter. However, this process will save you huge headaches in the future if your game thread is working too hard with the input, which a user might interpret that as a nonresponsive program.

Go ahead and fire up the InputTest project. If all of the code compiles properly, then you should be able to drag the sprite around the tablet screen. Because barely any physics or computing is going on in the background, there should be no appreciable difference in the application's behavior. When you add AI routines and dozens more sprites with backgrounds, you'll take full advantage of this slick way to handle input.

With these basic strategies for touchscreen events out of the way, you now examine the more exciting sensors that make Android tablets interesting.

Responding to Sensor Data

Android provides a simple way to acquire touch events, but sensors are a more complicated matter. This isn't to say that getting the data is tricky or difficult, but working with the input in a meaningful way can be a real challenge. You concentrate on accelerometer data here because it's the most commonly used sensor, and the other sensors (such as the gyroscope) are akin to it.

The data that tablet sensors deliver is very precise and usually of the Java long floating-point data type. This is a mixed blessing because long floating-point data is convoluted and complicated to figure out. Making things more difficult is the fact that tablets can be held in a variety of orientations. Holding the tablet in portrait mode completely alters the axis of rotation. To solve this temporarily, you can assume that the tablet is held in landscape mode. Later, you learn a way to detect the orientation of the tablet and instruct the user about the correct position for your particular game.

Let's add some code to the project and see what this sensor data is all about:

1. You need to import another Android library. To do so, add the code in Listing 3-13 to the MainActivity.java file.

Listing 3-13. Getting Access to Sensor Data

```
import android.hardware.Sensor;
import android.hardware.SensorEvent;
import android.hardware.SensorEventListener;
import android.hardware.SensorManager;
```

2. You may notice with these imports that you're talking about hardware-specific information. It's possible that the device that runs your game lacks the correct sensors.

3. Implement the SensorEventListener class in your MainActivity class. To do so, add implements SensorEventListener directly after the extends Activity line. When an error message appears, double-click it to create the two events shown in Listing 3-14.

Listing 3-14. Autogenerated Sensor Methods

```
@Override
public void onAccuracyChanged(Sensor arg0, int arg1) {
        // TODO Auto-generated method stub

}
@Override
public void onSensorChanged(SensorEvent arg0) {
        // TODO Auto-generated method stub

}
```

4. This is fairly self-explanatory: the creation of a `SensorEventListener` and then two methods that register when a sensor changes accuracy or its values change. You concentrate most on `onSensorChanged()` because you're looking for the data. There are many other functions besides these that you can use when you want very specific information from your sensors.

5. Place the lines in Listing 3-15 above the `onCreate()` method in `MainActivity`.

Listing 3-15. Creating Sensor Objects

```
private SensorManager mSensorManager;
private Sensor mAccelerometer;
```

6. Initialize these sensor objects in the `onCreate()` method, as shown in Listing 3-16.

Listing 3-16. Initializing Sensor Objects

```
mSensorManager = (SensorManager)getSystemService(SENSOR_SERVICE);
mAccelerometer = mSensorManager.getDefaultSensor(Sensor.TYPE_ACCELEROMETER);
```

7. To handle sensors, you add two basic methods that are already available with every activity: `onPause()` and `onResume()`. You need them here because you don't want to continue searching for sensor input when the device is already in some sort of sleep mode. The code in Listing 3-17 handles this issue.

Listing 3-17. onPause() and onResume()

```
protected void onResume() {
super.onResume();
mSensorManager.registerListener(this, mAccelerometer, SensorManager.SENSOR_DELAY_NORMAL);
}

protected void onPause() {
super.onPause();
mSensorManager.unregisterListener(this);
}
```

8. You can look at a modified `onSensorChanged()` to determine the values of the pitch, roll, and azimuth. For reference, *azimuth* is rotation around the z-axis,

pitch is around the x-axis, and *roll* is around the y-axis. To express the values of the accelerometer, you introduce a debugging technique for Eclipse and Android. At the top, import `Android.util.Log`. Then change `onSensorChanged()` to the code shown in Listing 3-18.

Listing 3-18. onSensorChanged (add import android.util.Log)

```
@Override
public void onSensorChanged(SensorEvent event) {

        float R[] = new float[9];
        float orientation[] = new float[3];
        SensorManager.getOrientation(R, orientation);

        Log.d("azimuth",Float.toString(orientation[0]));
        Log.d("pitch",Float.toString(orientation[1]));
        Log.d("role",Float.toString(orientation[2]));

}
```

9. Basically, you create two arrays to store values. Then you call on sensor manager to get the orientation of the device. Finally, you take the orientation array and print out the values. The `Log.d` function may look novel to you, but it's simply a way to send data to your debugger. Before you run the program, you can set up the view for reading these values by choosing Window ↗ Show View ↗ Other ↗ Android ↗ LogCat.

Now, instead of seeing the output of the console, you see tons of data points flashing by as the emulator starts up. When the application begins running, you see the accelerometer values. Figure 3-7 shows what happens when you use the emulator on a computer and it doesn't get any changes in motion.

Log				
Time	pid	tag	Message	
06–07 16:06 ...	D 370	role	−0.0	
06–07 16:06 ...	D 370	azimuth	0.0	
06–07 16:06 ...	D 370	pitch	−0.0	
06–07 16:06 ...	D 370	role	−0.0	
Filter:				

Figure 3-7. Noting the azimuth, pitch, and roll of a device

When I want to work with sensor data, I always test it on my actual tablet device because it's so simple to hold the device in different positions. If you haven't looked at it already, Appendix A has information about setting up your tablet for testing. If you're more adventurous or don't have a device, Android has a sensor simulator that can help you when you're writing code.

You can see the Google code project here:
`http://code.google.com/p/openintents/wiki/SensorSimulator`. It's actually a fairly easy proposition to set up the entire system, but I won't go into it here. At some point, only a real device can provide immediacy of response and show you what its processing capabilities are.

The Sensor Simulator does have some advantages over a real device. By correlating the exact movement values to the way the device responds, you can get a better feel for how well your program is working. For most developers, it's difficult to measure a perfect 37-degree rotation just by holding a tablet.

Using Sensor Data

To incorporate sensor data into the logic of a game and its updates, you need to pass the data into the game's View class. First add this to the MainActivity class:

```
GameView mGameView;
```

You must also add the code shown in Listing 3-19 to the onCreate() method:

Listing 3-19. GameView Instance

```
mGameView = new GameView(this);
setContentView(mGameView);
```

You now have a GameView instance from which you can call various methods. Next, in GameView, you need to add a new function to which you pass your orientation data to. Listing 3-20 shows the call to add within onSensorChanged().

Listing 3-20. Sending Sensor Data

```
@Override
public void onSensorChanged(SensorEvent event) {

if(event.sensor.getType() == Sensor.TYPE_ACCELEROMETER){
        float orientation[] = new float[3];
        for(int i = 0; i < 3; i++){
                orientation[i] = event.values[i];
        }

        mGameView.processOrientationEvent(orientation);

        Log.d("azimuth",Float.toString(event.values[0]));
        Log.d("pitch",Float.toString(event.values[1]));
        Log.d("role",Float.toString(event.values[2]));
}


}
```

The new portion of the code is the processOrientationEvent() call to gameview. Notice that you're sending the orientation data array to it. Listing 3-21 contains the code for processOrientationEvent() in GameView.java.

Listing 3-21. Processing Sensor Data

```
public void processOrientationEvent(float orientation[]){

        float roll = orientation[2];
        if (roll < -40) {
                sprite.setMoveX(2);
        } else if (roll > 40) {
                sprite.setMoveX(-2);
        }

}
```

Here you look at only the roll of the device. If it's low enough, then you want the sprite to move to the right. If the roll is high, then you have the sprite move to the left. To make this a bit more exciting, comment out the lines of the update() function. Listing 3-22 shows what that part looks like now.

Listing 3-22. Letting the Sprite Move Freely

```
public void update(int adj_mov) {
        if (sprite.getX() >= getWidth()){
                //sprite.setMoveX(0);
        }
        if (sprite.getX() <= 0){
                //sprite.setMoveX(0);
        }
        sprite.update(adj_mov);

}
```

Test this on your Android tablet device, and you'll struggle to maintain the sprite within the screen. If you desire, you can set the movement to zero when the tablet is held relatively straight. Here you use a very simple implementation of the sensor data, but in the final game project, you add a shake event that lets the user shake the tablet to restart the level. For now, you can play with the roll, azimuth, and pitch of the tablet data.

You must understand several aspects of sensor data to make them work. Accelerometer data is traditionally dealt with based on gravity. Therefore, when the tablet is still, the acceleration is still around 9.8 m/s^2. Many Android functions handle this for you, but if you come across functions that don't, you need to subtract out this gravitational influence. Looking up the Android documentation can help with this. Humorously, Android has built-in gravity constants for all the planets, including Earth. This way, you can adjust the accelerometer reading depending on the planet your device is currently on.

Finally, the coordinate axes are unique in that they take into account both magnetic north as well as the traditional dimensions. This means the x-axis is roughly from east toward the west, whereas y goes toward north and z points into the center of the Earth. The image in Figure 3-8 is from Android's own documentation on the subject.

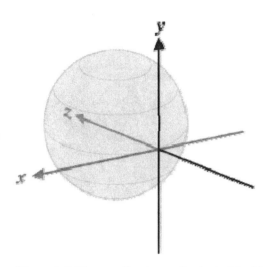

Figure 3-8. *The coordinate axes for Android tablets*

Because accelerometer and gyroscope readings are inherently in three dimensions, understanding matrices is very important for some of their data. To work around this, you should only ask for functions like `getOrientation()` where you understand the values to be an array of pitch, azimuth, and roll. You can experiment with even more sensor data by checking out the Android documentation here: `http://developer.android.com/reference/android/hardware/Sensor.html`. At the top of this document, you can view a list of all the sensor types that Android supports. Check out whether your target devices contain these before you implement them, though.

Summary

With the information about sensor and touchscreen input combined with the graphics work you've done, you can make your own game. Of course, there is still a lot of work to do in making the sprites interact properly through collisions and creating new sprite instances. You also have to deal with getting your game out to market.

Before you go on to any of those advanced sprite and development tasks, you need to understand the fundamentals of music and sounds for your games. When you think of tablet and phone apps, the music may rarely register, but that doesn't mean it isn't important. A game without sound is boring and leads people to attempt to run their music player in the background, which slows down your game. Android has created several fantastic libraries for creating interesting sound effects. You can take advantage of them to add excitement to your games.

C H A P T E R 4

Adding Sound Effects, Music, and Video

With a basic understanding of how to work with sprites and handle user interaction, you're much closer to a full, playable game. Now you add some elements essential to an immersive playing experience: sound effects, music, and video.

It's surprising, but many mobile games neglect sounds and music. Maybe the developers quickly added a couple of sound effects or put together a simple melody, but that's it. The audio portion of a game can really make your work stand out. There is no excuse for poor performance in this area, because it's one of the easiest Android game features to implement. The real limits are on what music you can create or purchase. Several sites already have taken care of this, though, by offering thousands of free sound files for commercial and noncommercial projects.

Video in mobile games has also failed to fulfill its promise. Much of this may be due to the small hard-drive space on handsets or the cost of data plans. Tablets, however, boast gigabytes worth of storage, along with the capability of quickly loading media from web sites and servers. You can use a quick movie to explain a game or entertain its player while the game assets load. Having a solid musical score and multimedia show for gamers definitely sets your game above the competition.

In this chapter, you create a new Eclipse project that incorporates sounds and media into your game. First, however, you address the framework that handles sounds.

■ **Note** In the past, game developers were hesitant to spend time and money on sounds because they believed mobile-game players wanted to be able to play quietly. With tablets, gaming has shifted to become a more multiplayer and social occasion where multiple people can enjoy the game simultaneously on the screen; therefore noise is no longer a concern. Games must still make it possible for players to turn off the sound, however.

Getting Ready for Sounds

Before you can explore sounds in your Android games, you need to find some to use. Android supports a variety of sound formats, the most popular of which are `.mp3`, `.wav`, and `.mid`. Personally, I prefer to use an MP3 file for small sound effects, like explosions, and MIDI files for musical scores. This is a common practice to keep file sizes to a minimum while also using the popular file choices. If you have sounds in other file formats, you can visit Android's list of accepted media formats here: http://developer.android.com/guide/appendix/media-formats.html.

Of special interest to some who have a passion for audio and music is the Free Lossless Audio Codec (FLAC) support that Android provides. FLAC is a format that is much like MP3, but it maintains the original quality of the sound. This is a great format to use if you have your own recording equipment or a collection of high-quality files. You can learn more about it at http://flac.sourceforge.net. Only Android 3.1 and later versions support this format.

Sounds and media files don't fit into the image resource files you currently have. To store them, you add them to a new folder named raw in your resources folder. This folder isn't created by default, so you make it yourself. *Raw* is the name you give to any media or miscellaneous file that isn't a layout or image file.

Now, let's locate some sound effects for your Android game.

Finding and Adding Sound Effects

Let's test some sounds; you can get a great selection online. Arguably the best resource is www.freesounds.org. You must first open an account at the site, but then you're free to browse its gigantic collection and download its sound files. The sounds are released under the Creative Commons Sampling Plus License. Basically, you're free to use them for your projects as long as you cite their licenses and give credit to their creators.

You won't find many full songs on this site, but there are sound effects for any possible game. For this chapter's example, I selected a spacey robot noise: www.freesound.org/samplesViewSingle.php?id=14259. It was uploaded by the user Harri.

If you examine the file formats on the site, the majority are .wav. You can use these just as you would as an .mp3.

To get started with a sound effect, follow these steps:

1. Download a sound file that you find interesting, and save it temporarily on your desktop or a place where you can easily access it.

2. Open the Eclipse IDE, and go through the steps to make a new project. Name it **SoundsTest**.

3. Open the InputTest project you built in Chapter 2, and copy all of its files into their appropriate folders in SoundsTest, including the star.png image and all of the InputTest.java code. Be sure GameView.java and SpriteObject.java are among the files you copy.

4. Close the old source code in the editing pane, and open the files from your new project.

5. To incorporate the new sound into the SoundsTest project build, you need to create a new file in its res folder. Remember that layout data and images are stored in this folder; but now you're dealing with a different file format that stores media files, so you use a new folder for it.

6. Make a new folder by right-clicking the res folder and selecting New Folder. Name the folder raw.

7. Find your audio file, copy it, and paste it into the raw folder. As mentioned, the raw folder is used to store resources like sound and video files.

Now you're ready to add some sound to a game. This process is similar in many respects to displaying graphics, but unlike images, sounds have a duration. Because of this, you use a simple way to play the sound once and let it continue.

Playing a Sound Effect

To access Android's ability to play sounds, you need to import the Android MediaPlayer library. Its name explains exactly what it does—it's used to play sounds as well as videos in your game. The class contains very few methods that you need to worry about. You see them as you work through the code.

Add the line in Listing 4-1 to the top of the GameView.java file.

Listing 4-1. Getting the Media-Playing Capability

```
Import Android.media.MediaPlayer
```

Listing 4-2 shows the code to create a media player object and then make a sound. Only two lines are needed to play the sound effect during the game. Instead of playing the sound when the game starts up, you'll have it play whenever a motion event is detected. Therefore, you add the bolded code into the function processMotionEvent; because you still have all the code that controls the graphics, you add the new code beneath the lines that reposition the sprite on the screen. There are some issues with doing this that you cover as soon as you've tested it: namely, your sound will be played whenever there is a motion, even if the sound was already playing.

Listing 4-2. Playing a Sound When a Motion Event Occurs

```
public void processMotionEvent(InputObject input){
        sprite.setX(input.x);
        sprite.setY(input.y);
        MediaPlayer robotnoise = MediaPlayer.create(getContext(), R.raw.robot_noise);
            robotnoise.start();
}
```

The MediaPlayer class is very similar to the SpriteObject class that you created. You initiate the object, and then you assign it the sound—or, in the sprite's case, the image. Then you're free to call its various functions, which in this example means starting the noise, while the sprite can be moved.

To see this in action, start the project and wait for the game to load. When you drag along the screen, you hear the sound played. If you're using the Android emulator, be careful not to drag many times in a row, or the project will crash from using too many resources to play the sound again and again.

Now let's see how you can manage several sounds, each connected with a specific activity. Almost no game uses only one sound; and whenever multiple sounds are involved, you have to deal with the possibility of playing multiple sounds at the same time. The next section goes over a class that makes this a simple proposition.

Managing Multiple Sound Effects

When you consider sound effects and the noise associated with a game activity like gaining health or shooting an object, you're looking at sounds that can occur simultaneously or at least very close together. The MediaPlayer class isn't well configured for handling tons of sounds that can be played quickly. To deal with this dilemma, you use a slightly more complicated class called SoundPool. Think of this class as an object that oversees the loading and playing of sounds in the background while the game moves on. It offers you several benefits over calling a MediaPlayer object.

Listing 4-3 contains all the code you need to update the GameView class to use the SoundPool class. It adds a large number of functions and procedures, so you need to be very careful that you write the entire file properly. When you run this application, it will function just like the InputTest application from Chapter 3, but with the addition of three sound effects that play whenever a motion event occurs. You use a simple counter to cycle through the available noises.

The new code in the listing is highlighted in bold. Be especially aware of the new packages that you implement as well as how the SoundPool works. All of this is done in GameView.java without manipulating any other class. Listing 4-3 shows the entirety of GameView.java so you can be sure everything is fine.

Listing 4-3. GameView.java

```
package com.gameproject.soundtest;


import java.util.concurrent.ArrayBlockingQueue;

import android.content.Context;
import android.graphics.BitmapFactory;
import android.graphics.Canvas;
import android.graphics.Color;
import android.media.AudioManager;
import android.media.SoundPool;
import android.view.MotionEvent;
import android.view.SurfaceHolder;
import android.view.SurfaceView;


public class GameView extends SurfaceView implements
                SurfaceHolder.Callback {

        private SpriteObject sprite;
        private GameLogic mGameLogic;
        private ArrayBlockingQueue<InputObject> inputObjectPool;

        private int sound_id;
        private Context context;
        private SoundPool soundPool;
        private int ID_robot_noise;
        private int ID_alien_noise;
        private int ID_human_noise;


        public GameView(Context con) {
                super(con);
                 context = con;
                getHolder().addCallback(this);
                sprite = new SpriteObject(BitmapFactory.decodeResource(getResources(),
R.drawable.star), 50, 50);
```

```
        mGameLogic = new GameLogic(getHolder(), this);
        createInputObjectPool();


        soundPool = new SoundPool(10, AudioManager.STREAM_MUSIC, 0);

        ID_robot_noise = soundPool.load(context, R.raw.robot_noise, 1);
            ID_alien_noise = soundPool.load(context, R.raw.alien_noise, 1);
            ID_human_noise = soundPool.load(context, R.raw.human_noise, 1);

        sound_id = ID_robot_noise;


        setFocusable(true);
}

private void createInputObjectPool() {
        inputObjectPool = new ArrayBlockingQueue<InputObject>(20);
        for (int i = 0; i < 20; i++) {
                inputObjectPool.add(new InputObject(inputObjectPool));
        }
}



@Override
public boolean onTouchEvent(MotionEvent event) {
        try {
                int hist = event.getHistorySize();
                if (hist > 0) {
                        for (int i = 0; i < hist; i++) {
                                InputObject input = inputObjectPool.take();
                                input.useEventHistory(event, i);
                                mGameLogic.feedInput(input);
                        }
                }
                InputObject input = inputObjectPool.take();
                input.useEvent(event);
                mGameLogic.feedInput(input);
        } catch (InterruptedException e) {
        }
        try {
                Thread.sleep(16);
        } catch (InterruptedException e) {
        }
        return true;
}


@Override
public void surfaceChanged(SurfaceHolder holder, int format, int width,
                int height) {
```

```java
        }

    @Override
    public void surfaceCreated(SurfaceHolder holder) {
            mGameLogic.setGameState(mGameLogic.RUNNING);
            mGameLogic.start();
    }

    @Override
    public void surfaceDestroyed(SurfaceHolder holder) {
            soundPool.release();
    }


    @Override
    public void onDraw(Canvas canvas) {
            canvas.drawColor(Color.BLACK);
            sprite.draw(canvas);
    }

    public void update(int adj_mov) {
            if (sprite.getX() >= getWidth()){
                    //sprite.setMoveX(0);
            }
            if (sprite.getX() <= 0){
                    //sprite.setMoveX(0);
            }
            sprite.update(adj_mov);

    }

    public void processMotionEvent(InputObject input){

            soundPool.play(sound_id,1.0f,1.0f,10,0,1f);
            sound_id++;
            if (sound_id == 3){
                    sound_id = 0;
            }

            sprite.setX(input.x);
            sprite.setY(input.y);
    }

    public void processKeyEvent(InputObject input){

    }

    public void processOrientationEvent(float orientation[]){

            float roll = orientation[2];
            if (roll < -40) {
                    sprite.setMoveX(2);
```

```
            } else if (roll > 40) {
                    sprite.setMoveX(-2);
            }
        }
    }
}
```

Here's how it works. You begin this implementation by declaring a slew of variables:

- Sound_id: Counter to determine which sound you need to play.

- Context: Means of getting the instance of the main activity to pass to your sound-loading function. You've dealt with this variable before.

- Soundpool: Unique object that controls the various sounds you play.

- ID_robot_noise: Integer value of the robot sound file.

- ID_alien_noise: Integer value of the alien sound file.

- ID_human_noise: Integer value of the human sound file.

You then initiate the soundPool object within the GameView constructor method. SoundPool takes three arguments: integer number of simultaneous sound streams, integer type of the audio stream (you use AudioManager to provide this value), and an integer for quality that currently isn't used.

The stream type is of note because you choose the most common option. AudioManager has other alternatives, such as STREAM_ALARM and STREAM_RING; they handle the audio files associated with their activity. A game will likely never need to use anything besides STREAM_MUSIC.

The next three lines load three different audio samples. When you create this project, you need to have three sound samples in your res raw folder that correspond to the resource id you pass to the load() function. The parameters of the load() method are quite simple: the first is the application context, and the second is the resource id. The final one is unused in Android's current version.

The load() function returns the id of the sound. This is then used to call the precise audio file you would like to play. Finally, you assign the sound_ID to the id of the first sound so you start at the beginning of your list.

Within processMotionEvent(), you have soundPool play one of its audio samples. The parameters are outlined here:

- Integer sounded: Specifies which sound to play.

- Float Left Volume: Use the maximum volume of 1.0.

- Float Right Volume: Use the maximum volume of 1.0.

- Integer Priority: Arbitrarily use 10. The higher the number, the greater the priority.

- Integer Loop: Use 0 to disable looping. -1 is for infinite looping, and positive integers refer to looping for that value plus one (for example, 5 loops 6 times).

- Float Playback rate: Normal playback is 1.0. You can go half speed or double speed with .5 and 2.0, respectively.

The next section of code increments the sound_ID counter and resets it when it has gone through the entire set of sounds. Also note that under onSurfaceDestroyed(), you call release() for your soundPool object to disband the object and clean up the memory it used.

To see how this works, play the application. Do the same dragging along the screen that you did before. A different sound plays every time. Then the list of sound effects cycles back to the beginning.

You can use this technique for a variety of applications in your games. When different monsters are destroyed, for example, they can play different sounds. The next section covers how you can play sounds when specific events occur.

Matching Sound Effects to Events

The previous example is all well and good for a cycle of sounds, but in most cases, you have a specific sound associated with each event. This is very simple to do and involves passing the correct sound id whenever you want the audio to be played. For example, imagine a situation in which the main character encounters a terrifying robot. You respond by playing the robot noise to alert the player to the new event.

Before you worry about the sound effect, you need to figure out whether the robot is near the character. To do this, you can create a robot sprite and test to see if the two are within a certain number of pixels. For this example, though, it will suffice to say that you have a way to detect this proximity. In your GameView.java update() function, you have an if statement that, if true, calls a new method to respond. Here is the pseudocode:

```
Public void update(adj_mov){

        If(near_robot){

                playsound(robot_noise);
        }
}
```

As you progress to develop an entire game, your update function will be loaded with different tests to determine what needs to be handled. Instead of playing the sound directly from the update() function, you may create a unique function like robot_encounter() to house all of your operations related to that event. For now, you need to quickly create a playsound() function.

Playsound() is actually a quicker way to use the soundPool.play() method. Listing 4-4 shows the code: add it to GameView.java.

Listing 4-4. Playsound()

```
public void playsound(int sound_id){
        soundPool.play(sound_id, 1.0f, 1.0f, 1, 0, 1.0f);
}
```

Wherever you wish to play an audio segment, you can call this function when you're in the GameView class. When other games need more sounds, as you need them you can create new sound ids that you can then pass to this handy function.

Without adding much code, you definitely increased the functionality of your game. Because sounds aren't rotated or moved like images during the course of the game, they can be initiated and then left alone. The new dimension you've added to your game will help users become more immersed in the game experience.

Adding Music

Music for Android is exciting. Some interesting technology provides amazing functionality. Before you look into these options, let's play a MIDI song file during game play. Your old friend the MediaPlayer class performs this perfectly because it's designed to play all the media files in Android.

Although music is generally longer than a sound effect, and you use a different file format, it's handled nearly identically to the sound effects in the previous sections.

To get free sound effects, you went to www.freesounds.org. For MIDI audios, I use www.midiworld.com. The site provides a large library of .midi files that you can use in your own creations. Under the Pop category, I found "Take a Chance on Me" by ABBA. Let's add it to your app:

1. Download "Take a Chance on Me" (or the song of your choice) to your desktop. Note that if you have your own MIDI files, Android is picky about using the .mid extension as opposed to .midi. In the future, Android may offer support for both, but this has been a common source of issues in the past.

2. Just like a sound effect, drag or copy the .mid file into the res raw folder of your project. Before you do this, give it a sensible name that is easy to retype. I renamed the file background_music.mid for now.

3. With the resource properly stored, you can look at the simple code that is used to run it. First create a private MediaPlayer variable at the beginning of the GameView class:

private MediaPlayer mp;

4. Add the following bolded code to the surfaceCreated() method. This is your way of instructing the tablet to start the music as soon as the screen image is created:

```
@Override
public void surfaceCreated(SurfaceHolder holder) {
        mGameLogic.setGameState(mGameLogic.RUNNING);
        mGameLogic.start();

        mp = MediaPlayer.create(getContext(), R.raw.background_music);
        mp.setLooping(true);
        mp.start();
}
```

5. Because you've already dealt with a media player, this code should be self-explanatory. The MediaPlayer object is created by loading the proper file and passing the context of the application. You do this to prepare the music for playing. You then tell MediaPlayer to loop the sample before starting it.

6. To clean up when you're finished, change the surfaceDestroyed() function with the following code:

```
@Override
public void surfaceDestroyed(SurfaceHolder holder) {
        soundPool.release();
        mp.stop();
        mp.release();
}
```

7. That's all there is to it.

8. Run the SoundsTest application, and you should hear music when the game starts. If you drag your cursor on the screen, the sounds from your soundPool play along with the music. You can use the method you've created whenever you want to play a music file in a game.

With the ability to play sound effects as well as music, you've finished your exploration of audio for Android games. The next important media object is, of course, video. The following section covers how to play a clip during a game. Because movies are media, they're handled much the same as sounds.

Adding Video

Playing videos during games is unusual, but they have a very important purpose in introducing games or prior to each level. Fortunately, videos are handled pretty much identically to music and other audio. In fact, to test a video, you can replace the .mid file with a .3gp file. Then, when the surface is created, the video will play.

Doing a quick Internet search for 3GP videos offers a plethora of options. If you have music videos in the .mp4 format, you can also add those to your raw resource folder. Listing 4-5 contains the code used for playing one of these files.

Listing 4-5. Playing a Video

```
@Override
public void surfaceCreated(SurfaceHolder holder) {
        mGameLogic.setGameState(mGameLogic.RUNNING);
        mGameLogic.start();

        mp = MediaPlayer.create(context, R.raw.intro_video, holder);
        mp.setLooping(true);
        mp.start();
}
```

Notice that the bolded argument to the create() method is different from the way you play sounds. This uses the SurfaceHolder that was passed to the surfaceCreated() function. Because a video needs a surface to play on, you give the video your SurfaceView to use. The video plays in the upper-left corner of the tablet's screen.

With that one quick change, the MediaPlayer is able to play a video. There is nothing else for you to work on in terms of playing the basic media types! You're now able to play sound effects, music, and video. The next section goes back to music and provides a brief introduction to *dynamic audio*. This is a neat ability that lets Android change the music that is playing based on changes in the game. You don't have to understand all of it, but it's definitely a unique feature that you may want to consider for your games.

Managing Music

Images in a game can be manipulated by rotating, transforming, and moving. In comparison, music is static: it can only be played and paused. In Android, you have ways to make music something that can be changed on the go. This is a fairly complicated technique, and it will probably be a while before you're comfortable enough with it to incorporate it into a game. Here you touch on the surface of the issue with a brief survey of the topic. Afterward, you can continue to explore for yourself and add it to your applications.

The goal of managing music this way is to create an even more immersive experience. When you watch a quality movie, the music changes based on what is happening. For example, as the main character gets ready for a battle, stirring music prepares you for the epic encounter. Slow, romantic music plays during a sensitive scene. You can achieve the same result in a game. The ideal result is that a game's music parallels the actions. When the player gets to a precarious bridge, for example, the music should shift to a foreboding tone. When the player approaches the end, glorious music pipes in. The game becomes much more immersive when the musical score isn't fixed but rather is fluid.

In this example, you use the JetPlayer class for this purpose. Like the MediaPlayer class, it can play MIDI files with a few extra features. It reads JET files that explain the procedure for playing various segments of MIDI audio.

Before you experiment with how JetPlayer works, let's see how to create your own JET content. The developers for Android created a beautiful environment for you to do this. It's called JET Creator; and to use it, you need to install Python onto your computer. Follow these steps to get it set up:

1. Download the appropriate version of Python for your computer at www.python.org/download/releases/2.7.2/.

2. Follow the instructions of the installer you downloaded. During the installation setup, you select a location where you want Python to be installed. See Figure 4-1.

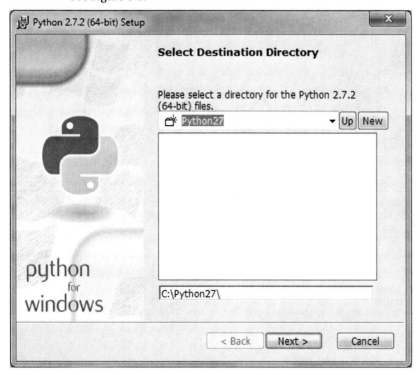

Figure 4-1. Be sure to remember where you place your Python distribution.

3. With Python properly installed, you need to install wxPython: www.wxpython.org/download.php. Again, select the version that is appropriate for your computer, and begin the installation process.

4. In the Setup Wizard, point wxPython at your Python installation, as shown in Figure 4-2.

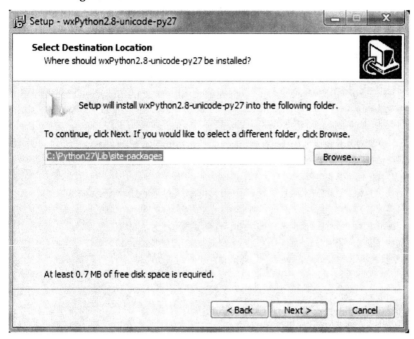

Figure 4-2. If wxPython can't find your Python installation location, you may need to point it at the folder Lib\site-packages in your installation.

■ **Note** WxPython is the tool used for a graphical user interface in the Python programming language. If you didn't have it, you would be forced to do all your work at a command prompt.

---

5. Start JET Creator. To do so, go to android-sdk\tools\Jet\JetCreator\ in the directory where you installed Android, and double-click JetCreator.py. A dialog box like the one in Figure 4-3 appears.

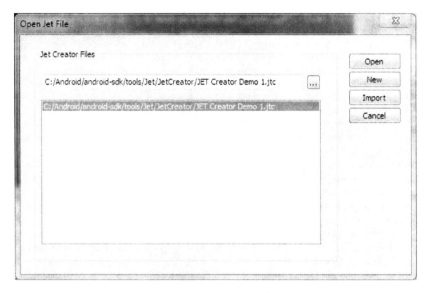

Figure 4-3. Don't worry if you don't see a folder path in your Open Jet File dialog box.

6. Click the Import button at far right in the Open Jet File dialog.

7. Find the path android-sdk\tools\Jet\demo_content. Select the ZIP folder named democontent_1.

8. When prompted, allow the folder to be unzipped in the default location, which is usually within the Jet folder.

9. You're presented with the JET Creator program, which lists several different MIDI files.

You can explore the JET Creator program yourself, but for now it's critical to know that each of the MIDI segments can be assigned a variety of events that trigger it. Events are the force that causes the music to shift from one piece to another. If you're really interested in creating your own event-driven music, then you need to become adept at using JET Creator. The best resource for this is the Android documentation available at http://developer.android.com/guide/topics/media/jet/jetcreator_manual.html. From there, you can edit the demo JET content and make it fit possible events in your own game.

Currently, your game doesn't have readily defined events, so let's look at an implementation of JetPlayer in an Android example project called JetBoy. After analyzing the code, you'll be ready to implement JET Creator in a future project.

To test this complete game, go to Eclipse and create a new project by completing the New Android Project dialog with the content shown in Figure 4-4.

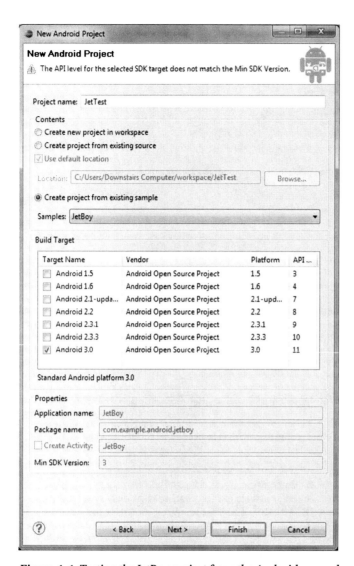

Figure 4-4. Testing the JetBoy project from the Android examples

With this project, you have several new files and objects worth paying attention too. Because this is a complete game, it's complicated; however, it isn't necessary to understand the entire thing. You only need to deal with how the JetPlayer class is implemented. Here's a quick breakdown of the files you're working with:

- JetBoy.zip: Found in the JetBoy_content folder. Contains the MIDI sequences and other information for playing the streaming music.

- Level1.jtc: Found in the res raw folder. Generated from JET Creator with the instructions for playing the audio.

- Asteroid.java: Asteroid class, which contains some variables.

- Explosion.java: Class that handles explosion variables.

- JetBoy.java: Main activity that pushes most of the handling of the logic to JetBoyView.java.

- JetBoyView.java: Largest piece of code, which works with the JetPlayer music content and runs the game engineer.

To fully understand this implementation, I have copied the important methods from the JetBoyView.java file to Listing 4-6. Following this listing is a brief explanation.

Listing 4-6. JetPlayer

```
private void initializeJetPlayer() {

    mJet = JetPlayer.getJetPlayer();

    mJetPlaying = false;

    mJet.clearQueue();

    mJet.setEventListener(this);

    Log.d(TAG, "opening jet file");

    mJet.loadJetFile(mContext.getResources().openRawResourceFd(R.raw.level1));

    Log.d(TAG, "opening jet file DONE");

    mCurrentBed = 0;
    byte sSegmentID = 0;

    Log.d(TAG, " start queuing jet file");

    mJet.queueJetSegment(0, 0, 0, 0, 0, sSegmentID);

    mJet.queueJetSegment(1, 0, 4, 0, 0, sSegmentID);

    mJet.queueJetSegment(1, 0, 4, 1, 0, sSegmentID);

    mJet.setMuteArray(muteMask[0], true);

    Log.d(TAG, " start queuing jet file DONE");

}
```

Here's how JetPlayer works. First, JetPlayer clears any previous files or sequences from its queue. This provides a clean slate for the next operations. Then it loads the file that contains the information it needs, which I pointed out earlier. Remember that this was created using the JET Creator application.

The starting sequence is set to 0. The exciting element is queueJetSegment(): this function loads the sequences of MIDI. It has a long string of parameters that serve to alter the audio, as explained in Table 4-1 from the Android SDK.

Table 4-1: queueJetSegment() parameters from the Android Documentation

Parameter	Description
segmentNum	Identifier of the segment.
libNum	Index of the sound bank associated with the segment. Use -1 to indicate that no sound bank (DLS file) is associated with this segment, in which case JET uses the General MIDI library.
repeatCount	Number of times the segment is repeated. 0 means the segment plays only once. -1 means the segment repeats indefinitely.
transpose	Amount of pitch transposition. Set to 0 for normal playback. Range is -12 to +12.
muteFlags	Bitmask to specify which MIDI tracks are muted during playback. Bit 0 affects track 0, bit 1 affects track 1, and so on.
userID	Value specified by the application that uniquely identifies the segment. This value is received in the onJetUserIdUpdate(JetPlayer, int, int) event-listener method. Normally, the application keeps a byte value that is incremented each time a new segment is queued up. This can be used to look up any special characteristics of that track, including trigger clips and mute flags.

Adding these segments makes better sense when you look at the implementation. Listing 4-7 contains the code for the run() and updateGameState() functions found in JetBoyView.java.

Listing 4-7. JetBoy Game Loop

```
public void run() {
        while (mRun) {
        Canvas c = null;

        if (mState == STATE_RUNNING) {

            updateGameState();

            if (!mJetPlaying) {

                mInitialized = false;
```

```
                    Log.d(TAG, "------> STARTING JET PLAY");
                    mJet.play();

                    mJetPlaying = true;

                }

                mPassedTime = System.currentTimeMillis();

                if (mTimerTask == null) {
                    mTimerTask = new TimerTask() {
                        public void run() {
                            doCountDown();
                        }
                    };

                    mTimer.schedule(mTimerTask, mTaskIntervalInMillis);

                }

            }
            else if (mState == STATE_PLAY && !mInitialized)
            {
                setInitialGameState();
            } else if (mState == STATE_LOSE) {
                mInitialized = false;
            }

            try {
                c = mSurfaceHolder.lockCanvas(null);
                doDraw(c);
            } finally {
                if (c != null) {
                    mSurfaceHolder.unlockCanvasAndPost(c);
                }
            }
        }
    }
}


/**
 * This method handles updating the model of the game state. No
 * rendering is done here only processing of inputs and update of state.
 * This includes positions of all game objects (asteroids, player,
 * explosions), their state (animation frame, hit), creation of new
 * objects, etc.
 */
protected void updateGameState() {
    while (true) {
        GameEvent event = mEventQueue.poll();
        if (event == null)
            break;
```

```
                   if (event instanceof KeyGameEvent) {

                       mKeyContext = processKeyEvent((KeyGameEvent)event, mKeyContext);

                       updateLaser(mKeyContext);

                   }
                   else if (event instanceof JetGameEvent) {
                       JetGameEvent jetEvent = (JetGameEvent)event;

                       if (jetEvent.value == TIMER_EVENT) {
                           mLastBeatTime = System.currentTimeMillis();

                           updateLaser(mKeyContext);

                           updateExplosions(mKeyContext);

                                           updateAsteroids(mKeyContext);
                       }

                       processJetEvent(jetEvent.player, jetEvent.segment, jetEvent.track,
                               jetEvent.channel, jetEvent.controller, jetEvent.value);
                   }
               }
           }
```

Although this code is tough, very little actually must be done to the JetPlayer; once the code has been added, other games will not need to make significant changes Recall that in the run() function, you have mjet.play(). This initializes any audio sequences that need playing.

updateGameState() triggers changes to the JetPlayer by changing the jetEvent. In this area, you also work with explosions, the laser, and the asteroids. Updating the current event is very easy: you cast the event into the JetGameEvent format. Finally, the last line calls the function that determines the music's response to the new event.

If you understand JetPlayer, then you're more than ready to implement it by editing the JetBoy game. If you're unsure about this code and how it works, don't worry; JET audio is a cool but nonessential aspect of Android's media capabilities.

Summary

In this chapter, you explored Android's multimedia capabilities, including the ability to play sound effects, music, and video. You also saw how these media can be incorporated into games.

It was a whirlwind tour. You continue to explore these features as you make your own game increasingly advanced. You can make your games more immersive through a proper implementation of sounds and audio as well as video.

With more exciting technologies to look at, let's move on to set up a more immersive experience for the game player in the next chapter.

CHAPTER 5

One-Player Game with Obstacles

After learning about graphics, sound, and input for tablet games, you have all the building blocks necessary for a simple game. In this chapter, you put them together, build a simple game, and ready yourself for some truly awesome creations. But to build even the simplest game, you need to be able to keep track of sprites, make them obey some basic laws of physics, and combine them in a way that engages the user in play.

In this chapter, you build a one-character game with some obstacles. The result is a simple game that is engaging for a player. All of this is accomplished through the use of sprites. Interactions between user and sprites along with sprite-to-sprite interactions make up the core of this chapter. The next section covers how to conceptualize your first true game.

Planning a One-Player Game: AllTogether

For your first playable game, you create a field of unexploded bombs and a character whose goal is to get from one side to the other without touching one off. To make the game more challenging, you set the bombs in motion. Let's call this game AllTogether because it incorporates everything you've done so far.

Before you get to the code, you need to do some planning. For example, here are some common elements found in most playable games. Not every game has all of these, but for the most part, you can expect them in a typical game:

- A user-controlled character (the protagonist) who faces the game's obstacles and challenges and must overcome them

- Dire consequences, which are the repercussions the protagonist faces as a result of failing to overcome the game's obstacles

- Rewards for success

These elements may look too obvious, but they're critical to being able to shape your game properly. Note that the first criterion isn't relevant for strategy games where the player controls an entire world. You work with a strategy game in Chapter 9, so you can see there how that is done.

The first item on the list is where 90% of programming comes in. If you envision your favorite game, almost the entire thing consists of the journey or quest to achieve certain goals and beat certain levels. The last two items are often very quick and merely serve to give the game meaning. Failure can mean running out of air under water, in which case your character dies. Alternatively, it could be that you're unable to complete the level quickly enough, and you must start over. Success is obvious when you reach the end of the stage or kill the final boss.

The game I created for this example has the first ttwo elements taken care of. You add the last one a little later in this chapter. To keep it simple, I wanted to create a game where the user must navigate three objects that are sliding up and down. The user must carefully time the bombs and then have the reflexes to run through quickly.

If the user hits one of the bombs, they're sent back to the starting point and allowed to try again. The game continues until they get bored and turn off the game. After looking at the original code, you add some features like the ability to display a victory message so the user can recognize their success. Take a look at the finished product in Figure 5-1.

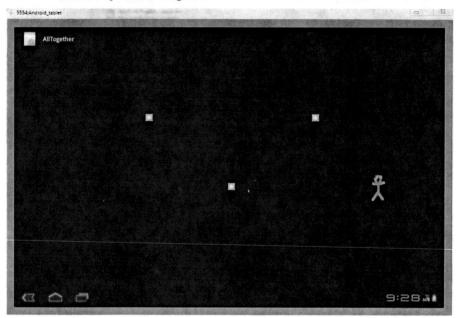

Figure 5-1. Beating the game

With this quick overview of the game, you're ready to make it a reality.

Building the One-Player Game

Because you've already done so much work in previous chapters, you don't need to change many things to build your first real game. The only files from the previous chapter that you must change for your one-character game are SpriteObject.java and GameView.java:

1. Open a new Eclipse project, and name it **AllTogether**.

2. Copy all the files from the SoundTest project in Chapter 4. Don't forget to copy both the Java source files in the src folder and the resource files in the rsc folder.

Before you start making changes, let's go over the procedure for handling motion and collisions.

Upgrading the Game Sprites

You begin by upgrading your sprites so you can more finely control their motion and detect collisions between them or with the boundaries of the game. This is a feature that will be instrumental in all your work from here on.

Adding Finer Motion Control

The speed you built into your last application is too great for your new game. To give you greater control, let's increase the precision of the variables that control a sprite's location and the size of each move.

You accomplish the change by converting the movement and location variables to the Java type double. Now, instead of being limited to integer values when you want to increase or decrease the speed of a sprite, you can increment those values by a decimal amount.

This ability is critical when you want slower speeds. The new game has movement adjustments of .5, which weren't possible previously—in Chapter 4, the lowest movement value was 1. To achieve this, you need to change the functions in the sprite class as well as the variable declarations.

To change the precision of your game sprites' motion and location variables, open SpriteObject.java and add the code in Listing 5-1 to the definition of the SpriteObject class.

Listing 5-1. Increasing the Precision of Game Positions and Speed

```
private double x;
private double y;
private double x_move = 0;
private double y_move = 0;
```

Next, you need some new code to detect collisions between objects. Collision detection is a key aspect of nearly every video game.

Detecting Collisions Between Sprites

The next big change requires an entirely new function in the SpriteObject class to deal with collisions. If you have done 2D collision detection before, the solution will look familiar. The function tests two rectangles for a collision. Recall that because the screens in Android have their origin in the upper-left corner, if the bottom of the first sprite is less than the top of the other sprite, then there is no collision because the first sprite is above the second one on the screen.

If there is a collision between the two sprites, then the new method returns true. Intriguingly, when you search for collisions, you use the bitmap to gather the width. Your sprite class doesn't store the width or height directly because it's already contained in the bitmap. You use this approach to get the dimensions of a sprite later for collisions with walls.

As with any function that requires a series of if statements, your collision detection is moderately expensive in terms of processing. You want to eliminate needless collision routines if possible. This is, however, much better than doing pixel-by-pixel detection that can cause games to reach a near standstill.

Add the function in Listing 5-2 to the SpriteObject class.

Listing 5-2. The collision detection function in SpriteObject class

```
public boolean collide(SpriteObject entity){
            double left, entity_left;
            double right, entity_right;
            double top, entity_top;
            double bottom, entity_bottom;

            left = x;
            entity_left = entity.getX();

            right = x + bitmap.getWidth();
            entity_right = entity.getX() + entity.getBitmap().getWidth();

            top = y;
            entity_top = entity.getY();

            bottom = y + bitmap.getHeight();
            entity_bottom = entity.getY() + entity.getBitmap().getHeight();


            if (bottom < entity_top) {
                  return false;
            }
            if (top > entity_bottom){
                  return false;
            }
            if (right < entity_left) {
                  return false;
            }
            if (left > entity_right){
                  return false;
            }

            return true;
      }
```

In Listing 5-2, you gather the x and y coordinates for each corner of both of the sprites. Remember that one sprite calls the function and uses a second sprite as the argument. It doesn't matter which sprites calls the function. The result will be the same: either true or false. Once you have the data, you go into four if statements. These examine whether the bottom of the first sprite is lower than the top of the other sprite. If this were true, then the first sprite would be above the other sprite and a collision would be impossible. The next if statements are similar in their checks on the position of the two sprites. If none of the if statements are valid, then there is in fact a collision.

Adding Multiple Sprites

The meat of your changes occurs in the GameView class where you make some major modifications to the updating functions. Creating an array of SpriteObjects called bomb[ ] is possibly the most important modification. Because the bombs all behave the same, it's much more convenient to group them this way than to deal with them individually. Doing so also eliminates needless code repetition.

The initialization of each of those new bomb sprites is also interesting because of their placement on the screen. The first and last sprites start out low on the screen, whereas the second one is near the top. This creates a staggered motion during game play to increase the difficulty. When you move to the surfaceCreated function, the first and last bombs move toward the top of the screen, and the middle bomb moves toward the bottom.

When you define the movement of the bombs, you're putting to use the new variables from the sprite class that can handle decimals. After doing some tests, I found that moving at a speed of 1 was too fast, so I halved it and used .5. To put your bombs on the screen, the onDraw() function uses a quick loop to cycle through the three bombs.

The update function contains the magic of the game. Here you define the relationship between the bombs and player as well as define the behavior of the bombs. The first two for loops keep the bombs from exceeding the bounds of the game; you want the bombs to bounce back and forth in a band between the y coordinates 100 and 500. The next for loop checks to see if your main sprite has collided with any of the bombs. If there is a collision, the sprite is reset at the beginning of the course.

Complete the update function by changing it to the code in Listing 5-3.

Listing 5-3. The new update() function to controll the bombs.

```
//check for bombs going too low
for(int i = 0; i < 3; i++){
        if(bomb[i].getY() > 500){
                bomb[i].setMoveY(-.5);
        }
}

//check for bombs going too high
for(int i = 0; i < 3; i++){
        if(bomb[i].getY() < 100){
                bomb[i].setMoveY(.5);
        }
}

//check for collisions with the sprite
for(int i = 0; i < 3; i++){
        if(spritecharacter.collide(bomb[i])){
                charactersprite.setX(100);
        }
}


//perform specific updates
for(int i = 0; i < 3; i++){
        bomb[i].update(adj_mov);
}
        spritecharacter.update(adj_mov);
```

Finally, the update functions for the bombs and the sprite are called. The processMotionEvent shown in Listing 5-4 also has some key feature changes. The two if statements look for events that signal the user has engaged and disengaged the screen. When the user touches the screen, the sprite moves forward. Otherwise, the sprite stays wherever it currently is on the screen. This method of movement is similar to the helicopter game where you attempt to navigate a cave: the helicopter moves toward the ground unless you tap the screen to make it go up.

Listing 5-4. processMotionEvent() method handles touches and releases

```
if(input.action == InputObjectinput .ACTION_TOUCH_DOWN){
        spritecharacter.setMoveX(.5);
}
if(input.action == InputObjectinput .ACTION_TOUCH_UP){
        charactersprite.setMoveX(0);
}
```

The code portion of your work is complete. Now let's work on the graphics involved in the game.

Adding Images for the Sprites

Your hard work is about to come to fruition. But you must add two resources to your project before you can compile it: an image of a bomb and a figure to represent the character (or player). They're both saved as .png files, and the character uses a transparent background so it doesn't look like a moving blob. The bomb dimensions are 30×30, and the character size is 70×120.

▪ **Tip** Don't worry if your graphics aren't impressive; the point is to have something to work with. Drawing on regular paper and then scanning the image is an easy strategy to improve your work. Touch up the drawing with a drawing program. Alternatively, learning to use a vector-based program can give your art a huge boost.

Compile and run this project in the emulator as you would any other app. If all goes well, by holding down on the screen, you should propel your character forward. If you hit a bomb, you start over. Enjoy!

The next section makes the excitement even greater by incorporating a reward.

Adding a Reward for Winning the Game

There are a couple of key points about the game play of this simple app:

- You added an obstacle in the form of the bombs. This was compounded by the quirky controls, which don't give the user precise movement.

- The repercussion for failure is returning to the beginning of the game. It's extra severe if you get caught by the last bomb.

- Having characters that resemble people has been shown to increase the interest of players. You did this by no longer moving a star around the screen as in previous chapters.

You can make this game better by providing a real benefit for winning. To do this, try making a sprite like the one shown in Figure 5-2 and calling its draw() function when the player reaches a certain x-value. Set a variable to true so the sign continues to be rendered, allowing users to bask in their glory.

This aspect isn't covered in the final code for the chapter because it isn't one of the core concepts. You're free to add it, however.

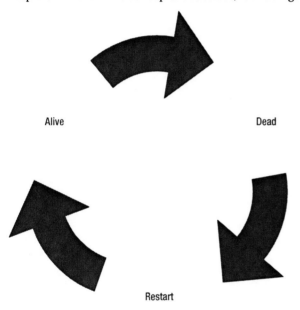

Figure 5-2. Rewarding the player

Tracking the State of Game Sprites

Because a sprite or an entire game can be in different positions or states, you need to develop a way to keep track of them. To conceptualize states, look at Figure 5-3. It shows a cycle of three different states.

Alive   Dead

Restart

Figure 5-3. The cycle of states

As Figure 5-3 illustrates, states are liable to change through the course of the game. Games go through life cycles as well, including startup, loop, and end phases. In Android as well as many other environments, states are defined as integers that can be accessed from various other classes.

■ **Note** You already used states when you were trying to find out what type of motionevent occurred. The if statement determined whether the eventtype was an up or a down action, both of which are integer values defined in the InputObject class.

All of this code goes into your SpriteObject class, where you handle the states of each sprite. Sprites such as bombs don't necessarily have different states, so you don't use these features for them. In your own games, you may prefer to create separate sprite classes that inherit basic features from the a high-level one and then differentiate the sprite subclasses with more specific methods and variables.

Follow these steps:

1. Create four basic states as integers at the top of SpriteObject.java (see Listing 5-5).

Listing 5-5. The constants to represent sprite states

```
public int DEAD = 0;
public int ALIVE = 1;
public int JUMPING = 2;
public int CROUCHING = 3;
```

2. My personal preference has always been to assign DEAD to 0 because you often have the default state equal to 0, and it makes sense to perform some sort of action in order to make the sprite alive (for example, initiating the level).

3. Another important aspect of states is that they should be exclusive. This means the character can't be in more than one state at a timeThe characters will always start out DEAD until they are initialized. From then on, they are ALIVE by default until an action is performed like jumping or getting killed..

4. You need to create two quick functions to work with sprite states. Put the functions shown in Listing 5-6 into SpriteObject.java.

Listing 5-6. getstate() and setstate() functions

```
public int getstate(){
        return state;
}

public void setstate(int s){
        state = s;
}
```

5. These functions should look familiar because this is exactly how you access the sprite's x and y coordinates.

6. Because the states that you define are public integers, you can test to see if a sprite is dead with the code in Listing 5-7 in GameView.java. Add this code to the update function.

Listing 5-7. Resetting the character if it dies

```
if(character.getstate() == SpriteObject.DEAD){
        character.setX(100);
        character.setY(400);
}
```

7.   Notice how simple it is to handle basic information like what is currently happening to the sprite. This become ever-more critical when you look at complicated states like jumping. Velocity is highest when a sprite first leaves the ground. It then gradually decreases until the sprite reaches its peak altitude, after which it gradually speeds up. The changing velocity of the sprite must be controlled within the update function. You need to find out what state the sprite is in, in order to change moveY at the correct rate.

8.   A normal jump, for example, lasts a predictable amount of time. But what if the jump is interrupted by hitting a platform? You use the state to quickly asses the new situation.

9.   To completely incorporate states in the game, put the line of code from Listing 5-8 in the if statement that tests for a collision between the character and a bomb. This is an alternate method for resetting the character's location when it hits a bomb instead of immediately doing it within the conditional collision test.

Listing 5-8. Starting the character as dead.

```
Character.setState(SpriteObject.DEAD);
```

All of this functionality is included in the code in Listing 5-9 and Listing 5-10. If you ever get lost, use this code in your project, and you should end up with a working game.

Listing 5-9. SpriteObject.java

```
package com.gameproject.alltogether;

import android.graphics.Bitmap;
import android.graphics.Canvas;


public class SpriteObject {

        public int DEAD = 0;
        public int ALIVE = 1;
        public int JUMPING = 2;
        public int CROUCHING = 3;

private Bitmap bitmap;
        private double x;
        private double y;
        private double x_move = 0;
        private double y_move = 0;
```

```java
        public SpriteObject(Bitmap bitmap, int x, int y) {
                this.bitmap = bitmap;
                this.x = x;
                this.y = y;
        }

        public double getX() {
                return x;
        }
        public double getY() {
                return y;
        }


        public Bitmap getBitmap() {
                return bitmap;
        }


        public void setMoveX(double speedx){
                x_move = speedx;
        }
        public void setMoveY(double speedy){
                y_move = speedy;
        }
        public void setX(int x) {
                this.x = x;
        }

        public void setY(int y) {
                this.y = y;
        }
        public void setBitmap(Bitmap bitmap) {
                this.bitmap = bitmap;
        }

        public int getstate(){
                return state;
        }

        public void setstate(int s){
                state = s;
        }


        public void draw(Canvas canvas) {
                canvas.drawBitmap(bitmap, (int)x - (bitmap.getWidth() / 2), (int)y -
(bitmap.getHeight() / 2), null);
        }
```

```java
public void update(int adj_mov) {
            x += (adj_mov * x_move);
            y += (adj_mov * y_move);
}

public boolean collide(SpriteObject entity){
        double left, entity_left;
        double right, entity_right;
        double top, entity_top;
        double bottom, entity_bottom;

        left = x;
        entity_left = entity.getX();

        right = x + bitmap.getWidth();
        entity_right = entity.getX() + entity.getBitmap().getWidth();

        top = y;
        entity_top = entity.getY();

        bottom = y + bitmap.getHeight();
        entity_bottom = entity.getY() + entity.getBitmap().getHeight();

        if (bottom < entity_top) {
                return false;
        }
        if (top > entity_bottom){
                return false;
        }
        if (right < entity_left) {
                return false;
        }
        if (left > entity_right){
                return false;
        }

        return true;
    }
}
```

We now look at the code in GameView.java that puts these newly empowered sprites into action.

Listing 5-10. The compelte GameView.java

```java
package com.gameproject.alltogether;
```

```java
import java.util.concurrent.ArrayBlockingQueue;

import android.content.Context;
import android.graphics.BitmapFactory;
import android.graphics.Canvas;
import android.graphics.Color;
import android.media.AudioManager;
import android.media.MediaPlayer;
import android.media.SoundPool;
import android.util.Log;
import android.view.MotionEvent;
import android.view.SurfaceHolder;
import android.view.SurfaceView;


public class GameView extends SurfaceView implements
            SurfaceHolder.Callback {

    private SpriteObject character;
    private SpriteObject[] bomb;


    private GameLogic mGameLogic;
    private ArrayBlockingQueue<InputObject> inputObjectPool;

    private int sound_id;
    private Context context;
    private SoundPool soundPool;
    private int ID_robot_noise;
    private int ID_alien_noise;
    private int ID_human_noise;
    private MediaPlayer mp;

    public GameView(Context con) {
        super(con);
        context = con;
        getHolder().addCallback(this);
        character = new SpriteObject(BitmapFactory.decodeResource(getResources(),
R.drawable.sprite), 100, 400);

        bomb = new SpriteObject[3];
        bomb[0] = new SpriteObject(BitmapFactory.decodeResource(getResources(),↵
R.drawable.bomb), 400, 500);
        bomb[1] = new SpriteObject(BitmapFactory.decodeResource(getResources(),↵
R.drawable.bomb), 650, 100);
        bomb[2] = new SpriteObject(BitmapFactory.decodeResource(getResources(),↵
R.drawable.bomb), 900, 500);

        mGameLogic = new GameLogic(getHolder(), this);
        createInputObjectPool();
```

```
            soundPool = new SoundPool(10, AudioManager.STREAM_MUSIC, 0);

            ID_robot_noise = soundPool.load(context, R.raw.robot_noise, 1);
        ID_alien_noise = soundPool.load(context, R.raw.alien_noise, 2);
        ID_human_noise = soundPool.load(context, R.raw.human_noise, 3);

            sound_id = ID_robot_noise;



            setFocusable(true);
    }

    private void createInputObjectPool() {
            inputObjectPool = new ArrayBlockingQueue<InputObject>(20);
            for (int i = 0; i < 20; i++) {
                    inputObjectPool.add(new InputObject(inputObjectPool));
            }
    }



            @Override
            public boolean onTouchEvent(MotionEvent event) {
                    try {
                            int hist = event.getHistorySize();
                            if (hist > 0) {
                                    for (int i = 0; i < hist; i++) {
                                            InputObject input = inputObjectPool.take();
                                            input.useEventHistory(event, i);
                                            mGameLogic.feedInput(input);
                                    }
                            }
                            InputObject input = inputObjectPool.take();
                            input.useEvent(event);
                            mGameLogic.feedInput(input);
                    } catch (InterruptedException e) {
                    }
                    try {
                            Thread.sleep(16);
                    } catch (InterruptedException e) {
                    }
                    return true;
            }


    @Override
    public void surfaceChanged(SurfaceHolder holder, int format, int width,
                    int height) {
    }
```

```java
@Override
public void surfaceCreated(SurfaceHolder holder) {
        mGameLogic.setGameState(mGameLogic.RUNNING);
        mGameLogic.start();
        bomb[0].setMoveY(-.5);
        bomb[1].setMoveY(.5);
        bomb[2].setMoveY(-.5);
         mp = MediaPlayer.create(context, R.raw.background_music);
        mp.setLooping(true);
        mp.start();
}

@Override
public void surfaceDestroyed(SurfaceHolder holder) {
        soundPool.release();
        mp.stop();
        mp.release();
}


@Override
public void onDraw(Canvas canvas) {
        canvas.drawColor(Color.GRAY);
        character.draw(canvas);
        for(int i = 0; i < 3; i++){
                bomb[i].draw(canvas);
        }
}

public void update(int adj_mov) {
        if(character.getstate() == SpriteObject.DEAD){
        character.setX(100);
        character.setY(400);
        }

        //check for bombs going too low
        for(int i = 0; i < 3; i++){
                if(bomb[i].getY() > 500){
                        bomb[i].setMoveY(-.5);
                }
        }

        //check for bombs going too high
        for(int i = 0; i < 3; i++){
                if(bomb[i].getY() < 100){
                        bomb[i].setMoveY(.5);
                }
        }

        //check for collisions with the sprite
        for(int i = 0; i < 3; i++){
```

```
                if(character.collide(bomb[i])){
                        character.setState(SpriteObject.DEAD);
                }
        }


        //perform specific updates
        for(int i = 0; i < 3; i++){
                bomb[i].update(adj_mov);
        }
        character.update(adj_mov);

}

public void processMotionEvent(InputObject input){


        if(input.action == InputObject.ACTION_TOUCH_DOWN){
                sprite.setMoveX(.5);
        }
        if(input.action == InputObject.ACTION_TOUCH_UP){
                sprite.setMoveX(0);
        }


}

public void processKeyEvent(InputObject input){

}

public void processOrientationEvent(float orientation[]){

        float roll = orientation[2];
        if (roll < -40) {
                character.setMoveX(2);
        } else if (roll > 40) {
                character.setMoveX(-2);
        }


}


public void playsound(int sound_id){
        soundPool.play(sound_id, 1.0f, 1.0f, 1, 0, 1.0f);
}


}
```

With all of those changes behind you, you've mastered the idea of states and also handled collisions and precise movement.

Summary

You've finally completed your first game. Congratulations! You also created code that you can use in future games. Adding sprite states is exactly the functionality you need to give your players much greater control over their characters. Almost any 2D game is now within your grasp to create. Your future projects will make heavy use of the efficient collision-detection method.

The next couple of chapters survey several different game genres that take advantage of the tablet's screen real estate, processing power, and input features. Chapter 6 covers a more complex game in which the player can use a paddle to hit a ball into blocks: the famous Breakout game. The major issue there is dealing with physics.

CHAPTER 6

A Ball and Paddle Game

In Chapter 5, you built a simple game in which a player dodged moving bombs. This gave you an excuse to use many of features and programming concepts central to creating games on an Android tablet. In this chapter, you build a more sophisticated game.

Your big task for this chapter is to build a pong-type game in which players use a paddle to keep a ball bouncing as they attempt to hit and destroy blocks with the ball. My first experience with a mobile game was on an old Blackberry where the only offering was this simple game. I had to control the paddle with the clumsy Blackberry trackball, and the small screen size and low resolution made the effort less than satisfying. Surprisingly, that game was written with the powerful Java language, the same one you use here to create your much more engrossing and fun game.

As you build the paddle game, you'll master new skills you can add to your toolbox. You add additional images to your resource files. You replace the character and bombs from the Chapter 5 AllTogether game with a paddle and blocks. To keep the ball in motion, you manage the interaction of the sprites and detect a greater number of collisions. You have to add some additional physics to the game, requiring more calculations on the fly. You also reward players more effectively with sounds and disappearing blocks. Finally, you learn a technique to initialize multiple blocks with a single XML layout file.

Let's get started.

Getting Started

Let's begin by gathering the images and other resources you will use in the paddle game, and then open a new project for your work.

Gathering Game Resources

Because a pong-style game uses fairly generic shapes and objects, you shouldn't have a lot of trouble making the graphics. The most important consideration, of course, is the relative scale and size of each of the elements. The paddle must be large enough to hit the ball consistently, yet small enough to make it a challenge for the player. You see as you go that other images can be added if you want to allow power-ups and bonuses to fall onscreen.

Figure 6-1 shows the images and dimensions of the graphics you use for this game. Notice that each of them is a different .png file. For my implementation, I drew them myself using GIMP, an open source tool mentioned in Chapter 2.

In addition to the regular graphics and sounds, Chapter 7 will incorporate the use of a new resource to store the layout of levels. Instead of coding in the position of each block, you specify it with an XML layout. This is the tricky part of this project, so I'm saving it for the next chapter. This first demonstration uses just three blocks without any additional resources for their placement.

Figure 6-1. The block (top image) is 30 × 50 pixels, the ball (middle image) is 30 × 30 pixels, and the paddle (bottom image) is 30 × 200 pixels.

If you're concerned about using a black ball (because the background has traditionally been black), have no fear. You can very easily change the color of the background. In fact, using a lighter color makes the game more inviting to the player.

░ **Tip** The paddle and ball images are partially transparent. You can do this by selecting the color white to be transparent in the GIMP program. I strongly suggest you do the same, because the game appears much more professional if you aren't dealing entirely with blocks. You're lucky to have the ability to use images with transparent layers, when other languages require code to make elements transparent.

This game is much more immersive if you have some nice sounds to go along with the game play. Because a pong game doesn't conjure a distinct set of sounds, you're can use whatever you wish. I chose to use only one sound: a short MP3 "twang" that plays whenever the ball collides with a block. The code doesn't include any other noises or music, but you're free to add them. When you start a new game, the simpler it is, the easier it is to find the errors and bugs in your code.

Creating a New Project

Because your game is complete (that is, it has user interaction, an objective, and the ability to win), you should treat it as a professional app rather than an exercise. Because of this, it's better to use specific names for the elements and code. Therefore, let's name this app TabletPaddle. Although not creative, this name describes your new take on a pong-style game.

To get started, follow these steps:

1. Make an Eclipse project with your name, and copy the code from the AllTogether project into your new project. Create a new folder in res, and name it raw to house the new sounds you add.

2. Upload your assets to their specific folders. Figure 6-2 shows how the project setup should look.

Figure 6-2. The proper setup for the Tablet Paddle project

3. If you get errors on the project initially, this is due to the absence of the graphics and sound files that the code is looking for. You fix this in the code when you work on the app.

4. Open the SpriteObject.java and GameView.java files in the editing pane. You can leave the other source files alone.

Now that you've gathered the resources and opened a new project for TabletPaddle, you're ready to code the game elements that you need, prepare the surface on which they'll be used, and adjust the game loop.

Preparing the Game Environment

Before you can work on the game loop for, you must initiate all of these new sprites—paddle, ball, and blocks—each of which has different attributes and properties. You also have to prepare the environment—the game surface—in which the sprites are used. Let's start by changing the source files you opened in the previous section to prepare the way for your new game.

Modifying SpriteObject.java

SpriteObject.java needs an extra function to return the MoveX and MoveY values, which are the variables that store the horizontal and vertical velocity of the sprites. In this way, you can easily reverse them to cause the ball to switch directions. In other game types, you may want to check the speed of a sprite to make sure it isn't going too fast.

Follow these steps:

1. Add the following two methods to SpriteObject.java:

```
public double getMoveY(){
        return y_move;
}
public double getMoveX(){
        return x_move;
}
```

2. You can make another change to SpriteObject.java to make the programming more convenient for you. Instead of worrying about the adj_mov variable that keeps the game at a constant rate, let's opted to let the game run as fast as it can. This avoids the hassle of dealing with very small movement values, and it adds unpredictability to an otherwise normal game. To make this change, go to the update() function, and change the code to read as follows:

```
public void update(int adj_mov) {
            x += x_move;
            y += y_move;
}
```

With those small corrections, you'll have a much easier time working on the game loop. You see the pieces come together in the coming pages.

Modifying GameView.java

Your game can finally take shape once you work out your processes and updating in GameView.java. Remember that this is where you store the code that changes the performance and functionality of the game. Here are the steps:

1. Because this game doesn't use the noises from the last game, remove these variable declarations from GameView.java:

```
private SoundPool soundPool;
private int sound_id;
private int ID_robot_noise;
private int ID_alien_noise;
private int ID_human_noise;
```

2. Look through your code and remove any references to these elements, because they will produce errors.

3. You also need to change the two sprite objects that your previous game used. The larger your games become, the more likely it is that you'll be using an array of sprites. This game is no different, and later you work on ways to populate your array of blocks with an XML document. You can remove the sprites from the last chapter because you have no use for bombs in this game! Declare your new sprites in GameView.java:

```
private SpriteObject paddle;
        private SpriteObject[] block;
        private SpriteObject ball;
```

4. Add the following variables, which you use to access the screen size when testing whether the ball touches the edges:

```
private int game_width;
private int game_height;
```

Note If all this deleting and retyping is bothersome, you can download a blank Android project through this book's website (http://code.google.com/p/android-tablet-games/). From there, you can create the game from scratch.

---

5. The constructor method of GameView must be completely redone to make your new app work. Listing 6-1 shows the new constructor method, followed by a brief explanation. Make sure your code is identical to that shown in Listing 6-1.

Listing 6-1. GameView Constructor

```
public GameView(Context con) {
        super(con);
        context = con;
        getHolder().addCallback(this);
        paddle = new SpriteObject(BitmapFactory.decodeResource(getResources(),
R.drawable.paddle), 600, 600);

        block = new SpriteObject[3];

        block[0] = new SpriteObject(BitmapFactory.decodeResource(getResources(),
R.drawable.block), 300, 200);
```

```
        block[1] = new SpriteObject(BitmapFactory.decodeResource(getResources(),
R.drawable.block), 600, 200);

        block[2] = new SpriteObject(BitmapFactory.decodeResource(getResources(),
R.drawable.block), 900, 200);

        ball = new SpriteObject(BitmapFactory.decodeResource(getResources(), R.drawable.ball),
600, 300);

        mGameLogic = new GameLogic(getHolder(), this);
        createInputObjectPool();
        setFocusable(true);
    }
```

6. If you look back at the last project, this should look very familiar. The soundPool object is removed from the code, and you plug in new coordinates for the sprites when they're originally rendered. Sometimes this can be tricky, so I like to create a blank image in GIMP that is the size of the screen (1280 × 1040). You can then gather the coordinates that look appropriate for your game.

7. The previous game involved three bombs, and here you basically replace them with three blocks. Obviously you want more blocks in the future, but this way you can reuse all of your for loops to cycle through the bricks. Because you're familiar with sprite objects now, notice that the only things you have to change are the location of the sprites and the image resource to use.

8. You need to get the ball moving. The next function that must be changed is surfaceCreated(), which you can simplify with only a few changes to the ball function. You also add two lines to assign the height and width of the canvas or screen to variables for use in your update function. Add the code shown in Listing 6-2 to the project.

Listing 6-2. surfaceCreated() Function Override

```
@Override
public void surfaceCreated(SurfaceHolder holder) {
        mGameLogic.setGameState(mGameLogic.RUNNING);
        mGameLogic.start();
        ball.setMoveY(-10);
        ball.setMoveX(10);
        Canvas c = holder.lockCanvas();
        game_width = canvas.getWidth();
        game_height = canvas.getHeight();
        holder.unlockCanvasAndPost(c);
    }
```

9. This starts the ball moving toward upper right, which should give the player plenty of time to track its movement and be ready to respond. If the starting speed you set here seems either too fast or too slow, surfaceCreated() is where you come back to change it, as you grab the speed from the ball object later on.

10. You also need to change the onDraw() function, but again it isn't a very complicated change. The loop to draw all the bricks is identical to the one you used to update bombs previously. Override your onDraw() function as shown in Listing 6-3.

Listing 6-3. onDraw() Function Override

```
@Override
public void onDraw(Canvas canvas) {
        canvas.drawColor(Color.WHITE);
        ball.draw(canvas);
        paddle.draw(canvas);
        for(int i = 0; i < 3; i++){
                block[i].draw(canvas);
        }
}
```

You've dealt with the basics. Now you move on to adding some bells and whistles to your previous work on collisions and events.

Adding Collision Detection and Event Handling

There is possibly nothing worse than working incredibly hard on a coding task and then realizing it was unnecessary. To avoid this issue, I spend a good amount of time diagramming and figuring out how the program will work and what it will look like. Figure 6-3 is a chart that shows what needs to be done and how the game loop must work.

If you're working with a team on your app, it's even more critical for everyone to share a vision for the finished project. This is when you may want to create concept art so that everyone has something to look at as they work on the code or assets.

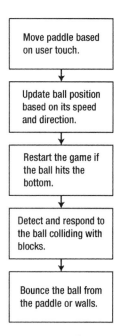

Figure 6-3. *The events that you must handle during the game loop. Each box represents anywhere from a couple of lines to an entire method dedicated to dealing with the changes.*

In your previous work, you tested for a collision and then reset the game. TabletPaddle adds a layer of complexity because you must respond to collisions in a variety of ways. On top of this, the reactions must be immediate in order to avoid strange behavior like the ball passing through the paddle or going off the screen.

The good news is that in this game, collisions with the walls, blocks, and paddle all cause the ball to reverse its movement. For example, when you throw a ball against a wall, it bounces back toward you. If you threw that same ball against a table, it would also bounce. Once you understand the concept, it's readily applied to all of the game elements.

Not all bounces, however, are created equal. Sometimes you need to flip the horizontal velocity, whereas other times you need to flip the vertical velocity. Alternating the *movement* of the ball means the *direction* of the ball. Your MoveX and MoveY values are in actuality vectors that, when taken together, represent the ball's speed and direction. Changing the sign of one of those values (making it negative if it's positive or positive if it's negative) reverses the way is the ball is heading.

Figures 6-4 and 6-5 illustrate how this works. The trick is to detect when the ball needs to change its horizontal direction and when it needs to change its vertical movement. This is the reason for the amount of code and the number of if statements you must use in the update() function.

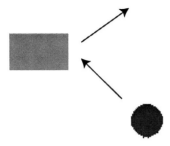

Figure 6-4. If the ball collides with the block from the right side, then it's deflected toward the right. Here the horizontal movement changes, whereas the vertical movement remains constant.

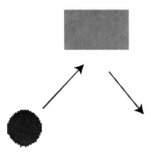

Figure 6-5. In this case, the ball hits the block from the bottom, and it bounces back down. Because the ball still moves toward the right, only the vertical movement changes.

You were able to figure out when two sprites collide, but you never specified which side of the object was hit by the other sprite. The code in Listing 6-4 deals with this problem by testing the x, y, right side, and bottom side of the ball against the paddle, walls, and blocks. Notice that you set the blocks to dead after they're hit, but you don't do anything to remove them from the game. This will be taken care of once you've tested your current work.

Listing 6-4 shows the code you use to modify update() for collisions.

Listing 6-4. Update() with Collision Physics

```
public void update(int adj_mov) {

        int ball_bottom = (int)(ball.getY() + ball.getBitmap().getHeight());
        int ball_right = (int)(ball.getX() + ball.getBitmap().getWidth());
        int ball_y = (int) ball.getY();
        int ball_x = (int) ball.getX();



        //Bottom Collision
        if(ball_bottom > game_height){
                ball.setMoveY(-ball.getMoveY());
```

```
                //player loses
        }

        //Top collision
        if(ball_y < 0){
                ball.setMoveY(-ball.getMoveY());
        }

        //Right-side collision
        if(ball_right > game_width){
                ball.setMoveX(-ball.getMoveX());
        }

        //Left-side collision
        if(ball_x < 0){
                ball.setMoveX(-ball.getMoveX());
        }


        //paddle collision
        if(paddle.collide(ball)){
                if(ball_bottom > paddle.getY() && ball_bottom < paddle.getY() + 20){
                        ball.setMoveY(-ball.getMoveY());
                }
        }



        //check for block collisions
        for(int i = 0; i < 3; i++){
                if(ball.collide(block[i])){
                        block[i].setstate(block[i].DEAD);

                        int block_bottom = (int)(block[i].getY() + ➥
block[i].getBitmap().getHeight());

                        int block_right =(int)(block[i].getX() + ➥
block[i].getBitmap().getWidth());


                        //hits bottom of block
                        if(ball_y > block_bottom - 10){
                                ball.setMoveY(ball.getMoveY());
                        }
                        //hits top of block
                        else if(ball_bottom < block[i].getY() + 10){
                                ball.setMoveY(-ball.getMoveY());
                        }
                        //hits from right
                        else if(ball_x > block_right - 10){
```

```
                        ball.setMoveX(ball.getMoveX());
            }
            //hits from left
            else if(ball_right < block[i].getX() + 10){
                        ball.setMoveX(-ball.getMoveX());
            }

        }
    }


    //perform specific updates
    for(int i = 0; i < 3; i++){
            block[i].update(adj_mov);
    }
    paddle.update(adj_mov);
    ball.update(adj_mov);

}
```

Before you start testing for collisions, you need to define the points of the ball. This saves you the time of getting the width and location of the ball every time you need to use the width and location of the ball. I suggest you do this whenever possible because it really clears up your code and makes it easier for others to read.

The next four if statements do the rather easy task of checking to see if the ball has hit one of the edges of the screen. The methods getMoveX() and getMoveY() that you created in SpriteObject are used several times because you want to invert whatever movement the ball previously had. Collisions with the side walls obviously change the horizontal movement, whereas the top and bottom cause shifts in the vertical direction of the ball.

You may have astutely noticed that you're merely bouncing the ball off the bottom of the screen rather than penalizing the player for it. This makes editing the game easier, because you don't have to worry about restarting it all the time.

Tip Often, when I create a game, I leave myself "outs" or cheats so I don't have to play my way through the entire game to test a single piece. For example, I don't want to battle through 10 levels of a game in order to test the final challenge; rather, I need to skip to that portion.

The code that checks for the ball colliding with the paddle may look deceptively simple because you only want to find out if the ball hits the top of the paddle. Although it's conceivable for the ball to hit the side of the paddle, this would only change the horizontal movement of the ball and still cause the ball to hit the bottom of the screen, which ends the game. To avoid needless processing, let's not worry about collisions with the sides. It's easier to see the concept without additional aspects.

The code for the paddle makes sure the ball is within 20 pixels of the top of the paddle. Because the ball can move only ten units in any direction at a time, it will never overshoot this window. Always ensure that this area exceeds the maximum movement of the sprites, so you don't have to deal with a ball or other item stuck inside another sprite.

Collisions with blocks are a different story. To handle the blocks, which must be capable of being hit from all sides, you have to do a little more work. The main point is that you first assign some variables to more easily access the block's location and dimensions. You then test first for the top and bottom collisions, which are the most likely. Then you test the left and right side hits. Notice that the order in which you look at the collisions affects the overall behavior of the ball.

Once one of the conditions is true, the game stops searching for more possible collisions. Figure 6-6 illustrates this concept. The left and right collision boxes are fairly small because you don't want to risk messing up a top or bottom collision.

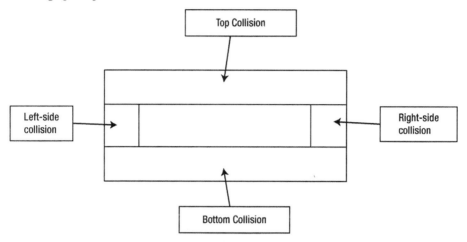

Figure 6-6. *Where the ball can collide with the block*

Adding Touch, Sound, and Rewards

Now you're ready to finish the application. You need to give the user control over the game paddle, and add sound and some payoffs to engage players.

Adding Touch Control of the Paddle

The AllTogether project used the touch and release of the tablet screen to propel the character forward. In TabletPaddle, the paddle moves horizontally based on the user dragging across the screen. You let the user drag the entire paddle around the screen for the purpose of testing collisions. When you're finished with the game, you can lock the paddle's y position by not allowing the user to drag the paddle freely.

Follow these steps:

1. Following is the new processMotionEvent() that updates the position of the paddle according to the position of the last finger touch. Change the code of your project accordingly:

```
public void processMotionEvent(InputObject input){
        paddle.setX(input.x);
        paddle.setY(input.y);
}
```

2. The code requires some minor cleanup as well. Do you remember the playsound() function and the processOrientationEvent code? Well, you can safely comment those out.

3. With the ability to control the paddle, you're finally ready to try TabletPaddle. Run the program as usual, and play the game. It may not be immensely entertaining, but it's a surprisingly functional game for very limited coding. Figure 6-7 shows the result you can expect.

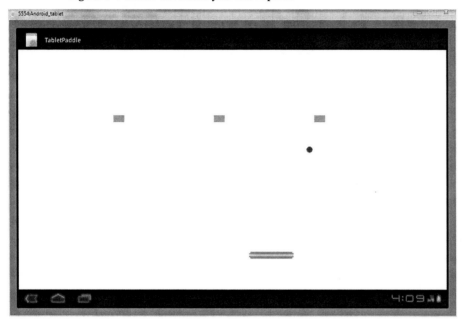

Figure 6-7. TabletPaddle

Adding Sound

The game can be played, but it's far from complete. The next order of business is to add sound to the game. You can do this by following the procedure from the previous chapters. Because you want only one sound, you can use the MediaPlayer class rather than work with SoundPools:

1. Add this variable to the variables list at the start of the program:

```
Private MediaPlayer mp;
```

2. Insert this code in the constructor of GameView.java:

```
mp = MediaPlayer.create(context, R.raw.bounce);
```

3. Listing 6-5 shows the portion of the update() function where you place the instruction to play the sound. Recall that you play the sound no matter what side of the block the ball hits.

Listing 6-5. Update() with Sound

```
//check for brick collisions
for(int i = 0; i < 3; i++){
        if(ball.collide(block[i])){
                block[i].setstate(block[i].DEAD);

                mp.start();
                int block_bottom = (int)(block[i].getY() + block[i].getBitmap().getHeight());
                int block_right =(int)(block[i].getX() + block[i].getBitmap().getWidth());


                //hits bottom of block
                if(ball_y > block_bottom - 10){
                        ball.setMoveY(ball.getMoveY());
                }
                //hits top of block
                else if(ball_bottom < block[i].getY() + 10){
                        ball.setMoveY(-ball.getMoveY());
                }
                //hits from right
                else if(ball_x > block_right - 10){
                        ball.setMoveX(ball.getMoveX());
                }
                //hits from left
                else if(ball_right < block[i].getX() + 10){
                        ball.setMoveX(-ball.getMoveX());
                }
        }
}
```

Instantiating the Blocks

With some noise going on, you can figure out a way to add a lot more blocks and make the game interesting. Instead of going through the arduous process of hard-coding the position of each block, you can put the x and y positions into an XML document. Android is very clever when it comes to storing data in another XML file. In fact, this practice is highly encouraged because it makes the code more readable and editable with only a slight lag in performance that usually isn't noticeable.

Here are the steps:

1. Create blockposition.xml by right-clicking on the values folder within the res folder and selecting new, then "File". Type the name as blockposition.xml. Following is the starting code to type into this new file. The goal is to keep the blocks in the same position but allow you to add more as you see fit:

```
<resources>
    <integer name="blocknumber">3</integer>

    <integer-array name="x">
    <item>300</item>
    <item>600</item>
```

```
<item>900</item>
</integer-array>

<integer-array name="y">
<item>200</item>
<item>200</item>
<item>200</item>
</integer-array>
```

```
</resources>
```

2. All this code does is establish an integer value of 3 that specifies how many blocks there will be. Then, two arrays handle the x and y positions of the blocks, respectively. When you add more blocks, update the blocknumber value, and add more positions for the blocks.

3. To access data stored in the XML file, declare these variables at the top of GameView.java:

```
private Resources res;
private int[] x_coords;
private int[] y_coords;
private int block_count;
```

4. You're using the Resources class, so add the following line to your set of imports:

```
import android.content.res.Resources;
```

5. Within the constructor for GameView.java, delete the lines dealing with the blocks. You're going to completely redo that portion. Following is the new and improved code that pulls the data from the XML document that you created:

```
res = getResources();
block_count = res.getInteger(R.integer.blocknumber);
x_coords = res.getIntArray(R.array.x);
y_coords = res.getIntArray(R.array.y);
block = new SpriteObject[block_count];
for(int i = 0; i < block_count; i++){
block[i] = new SpriteObject(BitmapFactory.decodeResource(getResources(), R.drawable.block),
x_coords[i], y_coords[i]);
}
```

6. res is basically your handler to call the functions getInteger() and getIntArray() from the XML file. The arrays and integer are stored, and then you go through a for loop, creating each of the new blocks. You no longer specify the number of blocks in the code, so it's very easy to change the number.

7. Unfortunately, you originally specified 3 as the number of blocks. Now you need to replace that value in the onDraw() and update() functions. Find those spots, and insert block_count where you see 3 in the for loops. The update() method has two locations where this change must be made because it calls the

update() functions of each sprite at the end and needs to check each block for collisions with the ball.

■ **Note** One of the reasons I like to store the layout and position of the blocks in an XML file is to be able to easily compare where each block is. For example, the three blocks that you use first all have a y value of 200. This makes it easy to slowly increment the x value because you can notice the trend in the vertical position. Because the blocks are 30 pixels high, you could make the next set of blocks at the vertical position y = 230.

Removing Dead Blocks

One major issue must be addressed before the game can be taken seriously: the blocks must disappear after they have been hit. You already set their state to dead, but you don't respond to the state in any way. To address this, you have some work to do in the SpriteObject.java file.

Basically, every function must have an initial if statement that checks its state. If the block is alive, then the action continues. If not, the function returns null and doesn't worry about the dead sprite.

Follow these steps:

1. Add this statement to the SpriteObject constructor to ensure that all sprites that are created are made alive. There is no use in initializing a dead sprite:

```
state = ALIVE;
```

2. Look at the code in Listing 6-6 for draw(), update(), and collide(). A simple if statement proceeds only if the sprite is alive.

Listing 6-6: draw(), update(), and collide()

```
public void draw(Canvas canvas) {
        if(state == ALIVE){
                canvas.drawBitmap(bitmap, (int)x - (bitmap.getWidth() / 2), (int)y -
(bitmap.getHeight() / 2), null);
        }
}

public void update(int adj_mov) {
        if(state == ALIVE){
                x += x_move;
                y += y_move;
        }
}

public boolean collide(SpriteObject entity){
        if(state == ALIVE){
                double left, entity_left;
                double right, entity_right;
                double top, entity_top;
                double bottom, entity_bottom;
```

```
            left = x;
            entity_left = entity.getX();
            right = x + bitmap.getWidth();
            entity_right = entity.getX() + entity.getBitmap().getWidth();
            top = y;
            entity_top = entity.getY();
            bottom = y + bitmap.getHeight();
            entity_bottom = entity.getY() + entity.getBitmap().getHeight();

            if (bottom < entity_top) {
                    return false;
            }
            else if (top > entity_bottom){
                    return false;
            }
            else if (right < entity_left) {
                    return false;
            }
            else if (left > entity_right){
                    return false;
            }
            else{
                    return true;
            }
    }

    else{
            return false;
    }
}
```

The only real trick to this is that the collide() function needs an else statement at the end because a value must be returned from the method. Otherwise you have integrated a very simple procedure that makes your blocks disappear as soon as they're hit. You can still access the x, y, bitmap, and state of the blocks, but there is no need to do so.

Summary

You accomplished a lot in this chapter. As it stands, TabletPaddle is a decent game that has a lot of room for development and improvement. The difficult and core functionality is present, the physics handles collisions fluidly, and the game responds quickly and correctly. I have compiled a list of some ideas to add to the game that may spark your interest. None of them involve Android touch programming, but they do involve logic and creativity:

- *Reset the game when the ball hits the ground:* Right now, the ball just continues to bounce. What if an image with the words "Game Over" appears?

- *Keep score:* You can detect when a ball is hit, so why not track the number of hits? Users can then see how well they're doing.

- *Add levels:* This task might be fairly demanding, but remember that the only difference between levels of this game would be the layout of the blocks.

In the `brickposition.xml` file, you could create sets of integers and integer arrays that store the location for the blocks within each level. After this chapter, you're on your way to making some killer apps. You learned some new skills as you worked through the ins and outs of handling collisions between a ball, a paddle, and blocks. You also covered some game logic and developed an intriguing way to handle complex collisions. In the all-important world of reacting to users' input, you provide sounds and make blocks disappear to reward users' work.

In the future, you increase the complexity of the tablet's actions. Specifically, in the next chapter, the processor will have a mind of its own. Instead of working only on the action of the player, the code can create events itself and make the player respond to unpredictable behavior.

CHAPTER 7

Building a Two-Player Game

You have done some fantastic work on games for Android tablets. Now you're going to add another level to the work by enabling one person to play against others who are nearby. This is a crucial step in making games that gather a huge following. If you look at the numerous popular games right now, the vast majority are played primarily for the ability to play friends and strangers from users' own homes.

Adding the functionality that connects multiple devices gets fairly complicated. Luckily, the Android documentation provides samples that you can adapt to achieve your goals, so all you have to do is understand how the code works and then incorporate it into your games.

In this chapter, you work on various aspects of multiplayer games including the different types and implementations. Then you move on to focus on Android specifically. At the end of the chapter, you'll understand how to create and adapt your own games for a multiplayer experience. Before you dive in, let's look first at the different types of multiplayer modes and how they are typically implemented.

 Note If you're confused about any portion of the code in this chapter, keep reading, and it will all come together. If you're still confused, check online for solutions or run the programs and change only the portions of it that you need to. The Android documentation is always a great starting place:
`http://developer.android.com/guide/index.html`. Often, it isn't necessary to be able to write all of the code as long as you understand how it works.

Understanding Multiplayer Games

Have you ever played a first-person-shooter game against others through a video game console or your personal computer? These games make video game companies hundreds of millions of dollars each year because of their ability to engage other players, not just computer-created characters.

Online games that involved entire worlds are also very popular (think of World of Warcraft). Tablets and phones are also catching onto this craze for more and more connectivity. Possibly the newest genre of multiplayer game is the social game. Farmville, Mafia Wars, and the various other products connect to social networking sites (most notably Facebook) to transfer information about your progress to the games that your friends are playing.

Multiplayer Games through a Server

All the games just mentioned involve connecting players through a server. This means the devices or players aren't connecting directly to each other but rather through another entity. In fact, web sites on the Internet use this same method: you (the client) get the web material from the web site (the server).

Figure 7-1 is a simple diagram that illustrates several people connecting to a server in order to play a multiplayer game.

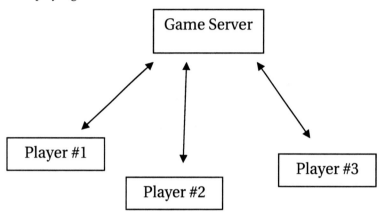

Figure 7-1. *A group of players from different locations log onto a central server and are then able to play against one another.*

Before you examine the advantages and disadvantages of server-type multiplayer games, it's helpful to be able to compare this approach to something else. Let's look at the peer-to-peer method.

Multiplayer Games with Peer-to-Peer

When players connect directly to one another, then they're using a peer-to-peer (P2P) network. P2P-enabled games played by opponents within a few feet of each other are typically implemented using Bluetooth, a local area network protocol available on most Android tablets. This means no entity is controlling all of the communications. If you've used a P2P file-sharing network (for example, using torrents to download large files from other users rather than a single server), then you've connected to other computers like your own to download files; you didn't need a large server to which everyone was connected. Many large video games for consoles don't use peer-to-peer because you would be limited to just a few players at a time.

To see the difference between a server-client game and a peer-to-peer game, take a look at Figure 7-2.

Figure 7-2. *Two players connect directly to one another in order to compete in a game.*

Obviously, these two strategies for multiplayer games are very different, but you may wonder which is better. There is no right answer; rather, there are instances when one is superior to the other.

Choosing a Multiplayer Method

Table 7-1 and Table 7-2 hash out some of the major pros and cons for the two multiplayer methods. This isn't an official list (and some people may disagree about whether something is a positive or a negative), but it gives you a very important grasp of how to choose your solutions.

Table 7-1. Server-Client Multiplayer Pros and Cons

Pros	Cons
Allows many players to access the game simultaneously.	Requires additional equipment and possibly fees associated with a server.
Reduces some of the computing for the individual devices.	A server crash affects every player.
Is much easier to update/fix.	The developer must write additional code to handle the server operation.
Players can be located across the world from each other.	Players can't easily communicate unless through an online chat.

Table 7-2. Peer-to-Peer Multiplayer Pros and Cons

Pros	Cons
Less code is required from the developer.	If a bug is detected, each player must download the updated version.
One device malfunctioning doesn't stop the game from running on the other devices.	The number of players is usually limited.
No need for server equipment (all of the devices contain the necessary technology).	The players' devices must do all the processing themselves.
Players are usually near each other and can talk while playing.	It's almost impossible to play against people across the globe.

If you've looked over these tables thoroughly, you should have noticed that the Pros column for the server-client method is the Cons column for the peer-to-peer, and the Pros for the peer-to-peer are the Cons of the server-client. However, adding up the pros and cons of each type doesn't lead to a correct choice. Instead, you must have a plan for what you desire to create and then select the method that best allows your goals to be achieved.

In the rest of this chapter, you adapt the Tablet Paddle game you built in Chapter 6 for two players, each of whom has control over one of two paddles displayed on their tablet. Because multiplayer programming can be complex, this chapter goes over the main concepts. The entire code is available here for you to work with: http://code.google.com/p/android-tablet-games/.

Because you only need to accommodate two players at a time, and you want to use the most efficient means of creating such a game, you use the peer-to-peer multiplayer game model. And instead of using an Internet connection over a 3G or Wi-Fi network to connect the players, you connect them directly using the Bluetooth network available on most Android devices. By choosing this path, you save huge amounts of time that would have been spent setting up server architecture and ensuring that devices could properly connect.

■ **Tip** For the beginning game programmer, it's best to stay away from server-client multiplayer games because they're nearly always much more complex. Don't be discouraged by this; you can create a plethora of great games from a Bluetooth connection. The added excitement for players in this case is that they're almost always near each other and can either talk each other through tricky levels or engage in some fun trash-talking.

Building a Two-Player Peer-to-Peer Game

As a developer, you can be reasonably assured that most Android tablet devices support Bluetooth. Nearly all modern phones support Bluetooth to connect wireless headsets for hands-free calling. This technology is implemented in tablets to allow for use of the same headsets as well as keyboards and various other peripherals.

Although some people use the term *Bluetooth* to refer to the headsets and the equipment they use to link to phones, in reality Bluetooth is a radio broadcasting system that devices of all kinds use to connect and share photos, music, video, and nearly every other type of data. The greatest advantage of Bluetooth is that it's incredibly fast. If you can make an uninterrupted phone call with a Bluetooth-enabled headset, then you can be assured that it will be fast enough for most games.

In the following sections, you adapt the Tablet Paddle game from Chapter 6 for two players. You first add code to connect two Android tablets using their built-in Bluetooth radios, and then you add a second paddle and code that allows the players to compete for control of the ball.

Let's get started. Begin by opening a new Eclipse project and naming it TwoPlayerPaddleGame.

Adding Bluetooth Connections

Because connecting multiple devices is a complex task, the code to support such interaction on Android tablets is trickier to explain. The snippets in this example were taken from a larger project on Bluetooth from the Android samples: BluetoothChat. You use them here to explore the main concepts. These variables haven't all been initialized, but they still convey the basics. Before you dive into the example, let's look through most of the elements that make up a successful Bluetooth application.

First, you must initialize your link to the Bluetooth connector within your tablet. Follow these steps:

1. Include the code shown in Listing 7-1 in the onCreate() function of MainActivity.java.

Listing 7-1. onCreate()

```
BlueAdapter = BluetoothAdapter.getDefaultAdapter();

if (BlueAdapter == null) {
```

```
    Toast.makeText(this, "Bluetooth is not available", Toast.LENGTH_LONG).show();
    return;
}
```

BlueAdapter becomes your handle to the abilities of Bluetooth in the device. The if statement is used to determine whether Bluetooth is available. The function then posts the message to the user, alerting they that they can't use the program.

2. Another portion of your startup occurs in a method that you haven't previously had to deal with: the onState() function that comes right after onCreate() in MainActivity.java; see Listing 7-2. You also need android.intent.Intent to be imported, which lets the activity send messages.

Listing 7-2. onStart()

```
@Override
public void onStart() {
    super.onStart();

    if (!BlueAdapter.isEnabled()) {
        Intent enableIntent = new Intent(BluetoothAdapter.ACTION_REQUEST_ENABLE);
        startActivityForResult(enableIntent, REQUEST_ENABLE_BT);
    }
else {
        if (game_running == null) startgame();
    }
}
```

The code in Listing 7-2 checks the Bluetooth device to see whether it's on or off. It starts an activity via a call to enable the Bluetooth device. (You very shortly look at what this new activity performs.) If Bluetooth is on, you check to see if the game has been started. If not, you call a new function that initializes the game. Note that much of your additional code revolves around the fact that many aspects of the game must wait for proper Bluetooth connections to be made before you begin.

3. The code in Listing 7-3 is used when the activity is sent a message.

Listing 7-3. onActivityResult()

```
public void onActivityResult(int requestCode, int resultCode, Intent data) {
    switch (requestCode) {
    case REQUEST_CONNECT_DEVICE:

        if (resultCode == Activity.RESULT_OK) {

            String address = data.getExtras()
                                .getString(DeviceListActivity.EXTRA_DEVICE_ADDRESS);

            BluetoothDevice device = BlueAdapter.getRemoteDevice(address);

            mGameView.connect(device);
        }
        break;
```

```
    case REQUEST_ENABLE_BT:

        if (resultCode == Activity.RESULT_OK) {

            startgame();
        } else {

            Toast.makeText(this, "Bluetooth failed to initiate", Toast.LENGTH_SHORT).show();
                finish();
        }
    }
}
```

This code above does two simple things. First, if you call it with a request to connect another device, it goes through the steps to gather the address of the other device and create a link to its Bluetooth device. Then it calls a new function in mGameView to tie the two devices together.

4. Now you have the very short and sweet startgame() function. Listing 7-4 shows how the game is started.

Listing 7-4. startgame()

```
private void startgame() {

    mGameView = new GameView(this, mHandler);
    setContentView(mGameView);


}
```

This function is largely unexciting, but it's critical to note that you're sending a new argument to the GameView constructor. The handler is your means of sending data from the Bluetooth channel to your game. Understanding how this works is possibly the most important aspect of Bluetooth programming.

5. The code in Listing 7-5 revolves around the handler that deals with the different tasks of sending and receiving data.

Listing 7-5. Handling the Handler

```
private final Handler mHandler = new Handler() {
    @Override
    public void handleMessage(Message msg) {
        switch (msg.what) {
        case MESSAGE_STATE_CHANGE:
            switch (msg.arg1) {
            case BluetoothChatService.STATE_CONNECTED:
                break;
            case BluetoothChatService.STATE_CONNECTING:
                Toast.makeText(this, "Connecting to Bluetooth", Toast.LENGTH_SHORT).show();

                break;
            case BluetoothChatService.STATE_LISTEN:
            case BluetoothChatService.STATE_NONE:
                Toast.makeText(this, "Not Connected to Bluetooth", Toast.LENGTH_SHORT).show();
                break;
            }
            break;

        case SEND_DATA:
            byte[] writeBuf = (byte[]) msg.obj;

            String writeMessage = new String(writeBuf);

            break;
        case RECEIVE_DATA:
            byte[] readBuf = (byte[]) msg.obj;

            String readMessage = new String(readBuf, 0, msg.arg1);

            break;
        case MESSAGE_DEVICE_NAME:

            mConnectedDeviceName = msg.getData().getString(DEVICE_NAME);
            Toast.makeText(getApplicationContext(), "Connected to "
                            + mConnectedDeviceName, Toast.LENGTH_SHORT).show();
            break;
        case MESSAGE_TOAST:
            Toast.makeText(getApplicationContext(), msg.getData().getString(TOAST),
                            Toast.LENGTH_SHORT).show();
            break;
        }
    }
};
```

Because this initialization of the handler does so much, following is a list of the various activities for you to see. You come back to this once you're actually creating your own project. Basically, the handler is passed a specific message or event that it must process or ignore. It has a huge variety of responses that you must code. Keep in mind that you send these from the GameView class:

- MESSAGE_STATE_CHANGE: The first case is if the state of the Bluetooth connection changes. For the most part, you alert the user if the state has changed into a nonconnected state. For example, if the service is attempting to connect, you alert the user of this. If, in an unfortunate event, the connection can't be established, then you also alert the user by explaining the issue. This is helpful in debugging issues as well.

- SEND_DATA: The next event is the need to send data to the other device. Here, you gather the string of code and are ready to perform the operation of sending it to the other device. You don't actually send it here; you come back and add this functionality later.

- RECEIVE_DATA: Similar to your call to write a message to the other device, you also accept the data coming from the other device. Again, this area will have more code later when you're sure what you want to accomplish.

- MESSAGE_DEVICE_NAME: The penultimate message is a call that simply alerts users about the fact that they're connected to a specific device. You alert the user through a small pop-up box.

- MESSAGE_TOAST: Finally, you have a generic way to send a message to the user from the GameView class.

Managing Bluetooth Connections

You're coming back to more familiar territory with some additions to GameView.java. Remember that you need to have the majority of the code here because this is where you can change the location of sprites based on the data sent back and forth between the tablets.

Listings 7-6, 7-7, and 7-8 show the code for three mini-threads that you must add to GameView to handle various Bluetooth operations that arise as the two players interact: AcceptThread, ConnectThread, and ConnectedThread. AcceptThread deals with the initial connection, ConnectThread handles the intricacies of pairing the devices, and ConnectedThread is the normal routine when the devices are together.

Listing 7-6. AcceptThread

```
private class AcceptThread extends Thread {
    // The local server socket
    private final BluetoothServerSocket mmServerSocket;

    public AcceptThread() {
        BluetoothServerSocket tmp = null;

        // Create a new listening server socket
        try {
            tmp = mAdapter.listenUsingRfcommWithServiceRecord(NAME, MY_UUID);
        } catch (IOException e) {
            Log.e(TAG, "listen() failed", e);
        }
        mmServerSocket = tmp;
    }
```

```java
    public void run() {
        if (D) Log.d(TAG, "BEGIN mAcceptThread" + this);
        setName("AcceptThread");
        BluetoothSocket socket = null;

        // Listen to the server socket if you're not connected
        while (mState != STATE_CONNECTED) {
            try {
                // This is a blocking call and will only return on a
                // successful connection or an exception
                socket = mmServerSocket.accept();
            } catch (IOException e) {
                Log.e(TAG, "accept() failed", e);
                break;
            }

            // If a connection was accepted
            if (socket != null) {
                synchronized (BluetoothChatService.this) {
                    switch (mState) {
                    case STATE_LISTEN:
                    case STATE_CONNECTING:
                        // Situation normal. Start the connected thread.
                        connected(socket, socket.getRemoteDevice());
                        break;
                    case STATE_NONE:
                    case STATE_CONNECTED:
                        // Either not ready or already connected. Terminate new socket.
                        try {
                            socket.close();
                        } catch (IOException e) {
                            Log.e(TAG, "Could not close unwanted socket", e);
                        }
                        break;
                    }
                }
            }
        }
        if (D) Log.i(TAG, "END mAcceptThread");
    }

    public void cancel() {
        if (D) Log.d(TAG, "cancel " + this);
        try {
            mmServerSocket.close();
        } catch (IOException e) {
            Log.e(TAG, "close() of server failed", e);
        }
    }
}
}
```

AcceptThread is a complex piece of code, but in actuality it merely waits for a connection to be accepted. Notice that the keyword socket occurs frequently. This is standard in any sort of connections between devices or entities and refers to the ability to exchange information. This code isn't mine; it's reused from one of the examples from the Android documentation. Several of it methods and blocks of code were incredibly efficient and required no redoing.

Listing 7-7. ConnectThread

```
private class ConnectThread extends Thread {
    private final BluetoothSocket mmSocket;
    private final BluetoothDevice mmDevice;

    public ConnectThread(BluetoothDevice device) {
        mmDevice = device;
        BluetoothSocket tmp = null;

        // Get a BluetoothSocket for a connection with the
        // given BluetoothDevice
        try {
            tmp = device.createRfcommSocketToServiceRecord(MY_UUID);
        } catch (IOException e) {
            Log.e(TAG, "create() failed", e);
        }
        mmSocket = tmp;
    }

    public void run() {
        Log.i(TAG, "BEGIN mConnectThread");
        setName("ConnectThread");

        // Always cancel discovery because it will slow down a connection
        mAdapter.cancelDiscovery();

        // Make a connection to the BluetoothSocket
        try {
            // This is a blocking call and will only return on a
            // successful connection or an exception
            mmSocket.connect();
        } catch (IOException e) {
            connectionFailed();
            // Close the socket
            try {
                mmSocket.close();
            } catch (IOException e2) {
                Log.e(TAG, "unable to close() socket during connection failure", e2);
            }
            // Start the service over to restart listening mode
            GameView.this.start();
            return;
        }

        // Reset the ConnectThread because you're done
```

```
        synchronized (BluetoothChatService.this) {
            mConnectThread = null;
        }

        // Start the connected thread
        connected(mmSocket, mmDevice);
    }
    public void cancel() {
        try {
            mmSocket.close();
        } catch (IOException e) {
            Log.e(TAG, "close() of connect socket failed", e);
        }
    }
}
```

This thread is similar to the previous thread in that it handles the attempt to connect to another device. The Android example also included this one, so I made no changes to it. If you're curious, it makes one attempt at *pinging* or making that connection with another device. If it fails, it can call for continued attempts via the try block, where a failure results in a restart.

Fortunately, you're really only interested in sending data back and forth and don't need to change how the connections are established.

Listing 7-8. ConnectedThread

```
private class ConnectedThread extends Thread {
    private final BluetoothSocket mmSocket;
    private final InputStream mmInStream;
    private final OutputStream mmOutStream;

    public ConnectedThread(BluetoothSocket socket) {
        Log.d(TAG, "create ConnectedThread");
        mmSocket = socket;
        InputStream tmpIn = null;
        OutputStream tmpOut = null;

        // Get the BluetoothSocket input and output streams
        try {
            tmpIn = socket.getInputStream();
            tmpOut = socket.getOutputStream();
        } catch (IOException e) {
            Log.e(TAG, "temp sockets not created", e);
        }

        mmInStream = tmpIn;
        mmOutStream = tmpOut;
    }

    public void run() {
        Log.i(TAG, "BEGIN mConnectedThread");
        byte[] buffer = new byte[1024];
```

```
        int bytes;

        // Keep listening to the InputStream while connected
        while (true) {
            try {
                // Read from the InputStream
                bytes = mmInStream.read(buffer);

                // Send the obtained bytes to the UI Activity
                mHandler.obtainMessage(MainActivity.MESSAGE_READ, bytes, -1, buffer)
                        .sendToTarget();
            } catch (IOException e) {
                Log.e(TAG, "disconnected", e);
                connectionLost();
                break;
            }
        }
    }

    /**
     * Write to the connected OutStream.
     * @param buffer  The bytes to write
     */
    public void write(byte[] buffer) {
        try {
            mmOutStream.write(buffer);

            // Share the sent message back to the UI Activity
            mHandler.obtainMessage(MainActivity.MESSAGE_WRITE, -1, -1, buffer)
                    .sendToTarget();
        } catch (IOException e) {
            Log.e(TAG, "Exception during write", e);
        }
    }

    public void cancel() {
        try {
            mmSocket.close();
        } catch (IOException e) {
            Log.e(TAG, "close() of connect socket failed", e);
        }
    }
}
```

The ConnectedThread class does an extraordinary amount of work. This code runs whenever the devices are in a connected state. Notice that it first gathers the input and output streams so that it can access the data from the other device and then in turn send its own information.

Next, the run() method goes into a loop where it constantly checks for new data that it can process. Most of your data is sent in the form of integers, but there are some benefits to sending strings as the interchange between the devices. First, in a complex game, there may be many numbers like health, ammo, location, and inventory that need to be sent. Just sending numbers isn't very meaningful.

Instead, a string like "a:10" can be quickly parsed to look for the number after the colon and the character before the colon to determine the change necessary.

Outside of the loop, the thread has a method that sends a message on the buffer to the other device. It's self-explanatory and sends the message as is.

Before these threads, you add some methods that are used to send data and call the threads to perform certain actions. Remember that you haven't yet initialized or utilized the threads in any way. The code in Listing 7-9 starts them.

Listing 7-9. Connecting to a Bluetooth Device

```
public synchronized void start() {
    if (D) Log.d(TAG, "start");

    // Cancel any thread attempting to make a connection
    if (mConnectThread != null) {mConnectThread.cancel(); mConnectThread = null;}

    // Cancel any thread currently running a connection
    if (mConnectedThread != null) {mConnectedThread.cancel(); mConnectedThread = null;}

    // Start the thread to listen on a BluetoothServerSocket
    if (mAcceptThread == null) {
        mAcceptThread = new AcceptThread();
        mAcceptThread.start();
    }
    setState(STATE_LISTEN);
}
public synchronized void connect(BluetoothDevice device) {
    if (D) Log.d(TAG, "connect to: " + device);

    // Cancel any thread attempting to make a connection
    if (mState == STATE_CONNECTING) {
        if (mConnectThread != null) {mConnectThread.cancel(); mConnectThread = null;}
    }

    // Cancel any thread currently running a connection
    if (mConnectedThread != null) {mConnectedThread.cancel(); mConnectedThread = null;}

    // Start the thread to connect with the given device
    mConnectThread = new ConnectThread(device);
    mConnectThread.start();
    setState(STATE_CONNECTING);
}

public synchronized void connected(BluetoothSocket socket, BluetoothDevice device) {
    if (D) Log.d(TAG, "connected");

    // Cancel the thread that completed the connection
    if (mConnectThread != null) {mConnectThread.cancel(); mConnectThread = null;}

    // Cancel any thread currently running a connection
    if (mConnectedThread != null) {mConnectedThread.cancel(); mConnectedThread = null;}
```

```
        // Cancel the accept thread because you only want to connect to one device
        if (mAcceptThread != null) {mAcceptThread.cancel(); mAcceptThread = null;}

        // Start the thread to manage the connection and perform transmissions
        mConnectedThread = new ConnectedThread(socket);
        mConnectedThread.start();

        Message msg = mHandler.obtainMessage(MainActivity.MESSAGE_DEVICE_NAME);
        Bundle bundle = new Bundle();
        bundle.putString(BluetoothChat.DEVICE_NAME, device.getName());
        msg.setData(bundle);
        mHandler.sendMessage(msg);

        setState(STATE_CONNECTED);
    }

    public synchronized void stop() {
        if (D) Log.d(TAG, "stop");
        if (mConnectThread != null) {mConnectThread.cancel(); mConnectThread = null;}
        if (mConnectedThread != null) {mConnectedThread.cancel(); mConnectedThread = null;}
        if (mAcceptThread != null) {mAcceptThread.cancel(); mAcceptThread = null;}
        setState(STATE_NONE);
    }

    public void write(byte[] out) {
        // Create temporary object
        ConnectedThread r;
        // Synchronize a copy of the ConnectedThread
        synchronized (this) {
            if (mState != STATE_CONNECTED) return;
            r = mConnectedThread;
        }
        // Perform the write unsynchronized
        r.write(out);
    }

    private void connectionFailed() {
        setState(STATE_LISTEN);

        // Send a failure message back to the Activity
        Message msg = mHandler.obtainMessage(MainActivity.MESSAGE_TOAST);
        Bundle bundle = new Bundle();
        bundle.putString(BluetoothChat.TOAST, "Unable to connect device");
        msg.setData(bundle);
        mHandler.sendMessage(msg);
    }

    private void connectionLost() {
        setState(STATE_LISTEN);

        // Send a failure message back to the Activity
        Message msg = mHandler.obtainMessage(MainActivity.MESSAGE_TOAST);
```

```
Bundle bundle = new Bundle();
bundle.putString(MainActivity.TOAST, "Device connection was lost");
msg.setData(bundle);
mHandler.sendMessage(msg);
}
```

Once you've seen the threads, you understand that these functions mainly work to start the threads. The first three functions start the three threads (AcceptThread, ConnectThread, and ConnectedThread). When your game encounters the end (that is, the character dies), the stop() function is called to make sure none of the threads continue. You also use the write() method when you wish to send something to the other device.

Finally, the other two methods use the Handler to display messages when the connection is lost or fails.

Adapting the Game Code for Two Players

You got through the majority of the code that deals with setting up connections and then maintaining them. Now you need to figure out how your game will work with the Bluetooth. The entire code for this sample game was much too large to fit into the pages of this book, but you can download it from http://code.google.com/p/android-tablet-games/. An entire other source file handles how you pick which device you want to connect to (that isn't important to your work right now).

Without further ado, you want to have two paddles on the screen during the game: one at the top and one at the bottom. Listing 7-10 contains the important code from the update() method of GameView. Note that you have to initialize the paddle_other sprite in the previous functions and add it to the draw() function as well. It's placed at the top of the screen with the same image as the other paddle.

Listing 7-10. Adding a Paddle and Collision Detection, and Updating Game State

```
//paddle input
int val=0;
for (int i=latest_input.length-1, j = 0; i >= 0; i--,j++)
        {
                val += (latest_input[i] & 0xff) << (8*j);
        }
paddle_other.setX(val);

//paddle_other collision
int paddle_other_bottom = paddle_other.getBitmap().getHeight();
if(paddle_other.collide(ball)){
        if(ball_y < paddle_other_bottom && ball_y < paddle_other_bottom + 20){
                ball.setMoveY(-ball.getMoveY());
        }
}

//paddle output
byte[] paddle_output;
ByteBuffer bb = ByteBuffer.allocate(4);
bb.putInt((int)paddle.getX());
paddle_output = bb.array();
write(paddle_output);
```

The code in Listing 7-10 does three things. First, it moves paddle_other to the location based on the input from the other device that is controlling it. Second, it detects collisions. Third, it sends the location of the paddle that you control to the other device so your opponent can see your latest move.

Breaking it down a little, the for loop converts the byte array you get as input into an integer for moving the paddle. Luckily, you don't yet have to parse byte[] into more complex values.

The collision detection is similar to that for the other paddle, but you invert the detection because you're only interested in the ball hitting the bottom, not the top. If you desire, you can cause the game to reset or end when the ball touches the top, to put the same level of intensity on player 2.

Finally, you convert the location of the paddle to a byte array and send it into your write() function, which in turn sends it to the connectedThread where it's dealt with.

Testing the Game

Testing a multiplayer game application that uses Bluetooth can be a bit tricky. If you have two Android tablets, then you can use their built-in ability to tether to each other. Then load the program onto both of devices. If you don't own or want several tablets, you must make different arrangements.

Obviously, another possible way to test these programs is to borrow someone else's tablet and pair it with your own. Note that to install software on another tablet, you need to follow the instructions in Appendix A for all tablets. Make sure your friends or relatives understand what you're doing to their tablet before you embark on your experiments!

It may be tempting to plug a Bluetooth USB dongle into your computer and expect your emulator to be able to handle Bluetooth. Sadly, this isn't the case; the emulator currently doesn't have the ability to deal with Bluetooth. Until this functionality is added, you must use real devices for testing.

Summary

Congratulations once again: you fought your way through some interesting Bluetooth and multiplayer aspects of Android game development. This topic is one of the more difficult that you'll encounter in your game programming. Now you're ready to work on the massive game at the end of this book. Get ready for more sprites and sounds, and a lot more code.

CHAPTER 8

A One-Player Strategy Game

Part I: Building the Game

It's time to work on your final game, a one-player strategy game—Harbor Defender—for which you use the concepts and code you've developed in the earlier chapters. Most of the content is stuff that we have already learned. You make use of what you already know. Some game-development books like to end with a flashy 3D game. I chose not to take this route because there isn't enough time to teach you all the nuances of adding a third dimension. Writing a 3D game isn't easy: when you play one on your smartphone or tablet, you can be fairly certain that it was created by a large team. My goal in this book is to teach you how to create games that you can program by yourself. This way, you won't have to share your profits with anyone, nor will you have to argue with fellow developers about your design and implementation decisions!

In the strategy game you build, the user must defend a fortress from enemies that attack from the sea. The design of the game allows you to increase its difficulty by adding new types of defenses and increasing the number of enemies. It's also possible to add layouts to create more challenging levels of play.

In this chapter, the first of two, you focus on setting up the game and its elements and on creating a system that makes everything run smoothly. In the next chapter, you polish the game by implementing a point counter as well as some intriguing user controls that give the game more excitement.

Note Because you're building a game for a tablet, you need to keep in mind the aspects that make its development different from a phone or desktop game. Such differences include using a touchscreen, coping with screen sizes, and designing user controls that are intuitive. Some developers new to tablets are tempted to port their previous projects to the device. This can work well, but a look through the app store will convince you that most of the games there are customized for the tablet and wouldn't work well on any other hardware. Very often, users just play the original on their game system, and they're expecting a special game for their tablet experience.

Let's begin by taking a look at the layout of the strategy game and then assembling the elements required to build it.

Introducing Harbor Defender

Harbor Defender is the name I've chosen for the game you begin in this chapter. The game surface consists of a fortress, a harbor defined by a pier, attacking boats, and cannons that can sink the attackers with bullets. Figure 8-1 is an image of the game surface you assemble by the end of this chapter. In Chapter 9 you add the user controls, but for now you need a surface that the player will eventually interact with. It gives you an idea how the mechanics will work.

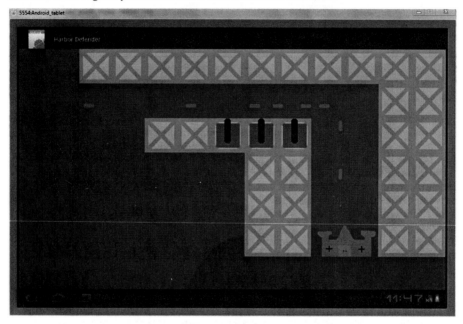

Figure 8-1. The beta version of Harbor Defender

The object of Harbor Defender is to destroy ships approaching the fortress through the harbor before they can invade it. The player repels the boats by firing cannons located on the pier that encloses the harbor. Each of the pier pieces can hold one cannon, but the user must aim it in the proper direction. To make the game more challenging, users can't create an unlimited number of cannons. Rather, users are given a limited number of cannons, and they must therefore be judicious in the cannons' placement. As mentioned, in this chapter you set up the game environment; in the next chapter you add user interaction.

You can make the boats approach at increasing rates later, and the user will have to quickly delete and move cannons in order to maximize their efficiency. Now, let's look at the items and activities that you must create in order to make this game a success.

Assembling Harbor Defender

Here is a breakdown of what Harbor Defender entails. In this section you explore these elements and how to handle them:

- *The pier:* The blocks of the pier support your cannons and define the harbor through which the invading boats must navigate. The pier itself doesn't do anything, but it's used when referencing cannon placement. You use XML data to quickly code the location of each and every piece. Each piece is implemented as a sprite; sprite objects give you much more functionality than merely putting images on the screen.

- *Ground:* The ground is part of the background, and you don't test it or use it. It's important, however, that you use it because it saves you from having to use a much larger and resource-intensive image when the blue background suffices.

- *Castle:* The castle only reacts if a boat strikes it. Otherwise, it's an immovable object that is relatively simple to implement. Again, you could have chosen to make the ground and castle into one sprite, but you use this method because it makes more sense within the game by limiting the size of images.

- *Boats:* The boats are one of the only two moving sprites in the entire game. You create them based on a random number generator to add some unpredictability to the game. You also preprogram their route and speed. The bullets are another moving sprite that you handle in Chapter 9.

- *Cannons:* The cannons have a simple function, and that is to fire on the boats. Their placement is unique because the user can create and destroy cannons during the game. Again, the functionality of the cannons is implemented in the next chapter.

The most intriguing portion of the coding of this game is the idea that the boats and cannons don't have a set location or number. This means not all of the sprites are initialized at the beginning as you're used to.

Before you begin to build your game environment, you need to open a new Eclipse project:

1. Open a new Eclipse project, and name it **HarborDefender**.

2. Copy all the files of PaddleGame (see Chapter 7) to your new project. This includes the art, XML files, and of course the code.

Constructing the Pier

In your last game, you used an XML page to store the location of the blocks. You reuse this page to store the vast number of pier coordinates. Because you have so many piers, some would argue that a loop could handle the quick arrangement of the pieces. This is true, but the irregular shape of the pier lends itself to this sort of manual coding. Also, remember that if you create another level, it's very easy to change this data.

Follow these steps:

1. Listing 8-1 shows the contents of the file blocklocation.xml (the exact same one you used for TabletPaddle), but it contains the location of all of the pier pieces rather than the blocks from the paddle game. Add the contents of this file to blocklocation.xml, which is located under res values. Instead of typing this code in, I highly recommend downloading the file from the web site (http://code.google.com/p/android-tablet-games/).

Listing 8-1. Pier Platform Locations

```xml
<resources>
    <integer name="blocknumber">32</integer>

    <integer-array name="x">

    <item>180</item>
    <item>280</item>
    <item>380</item>
    <item>480</item>
    <item>580</item>
    <item>680</item>
    <item>780</item>
    <item>880</item>
    <item>980</item>
    <item>1080</item>
    <item>1180</item>
    <item>1080</item>
    <item>1180</item>
    <item>380</item>
    <item>480</item>
    <item>580</item>
    <item>680</item>
    <item>780</item>
    <item>1080</item>
    <item>1180</item>
    <item>680</item>
    <item>780</item>
    <item>1080</item>
    <item>1180</item>
    <item>680</item>
    <item>780</item>
    <item>1080</item>
    <item>1180</item>
    <item>680</item>
    <item>780</item>
    <item>1080</item>
    <item>1180</item>

    </integer-array>

    <integer-array name="y">

    <item>0</item>
    <item>0</item>
    <item>0</item>
    <item>0</item>
    <item>0</item>
    <item>0</item>
    <item>0</item>
```

```
     <item>0</item>
     <item>0</item>
     <item>0</item>
     <item>0</item>
     <item>100</item>
     <item>100</item>
     <item>200</item>
     <item>200</item>
     <item>200</item>
     <item>200</item>
     <item>200</item>
     <item>200</item>
     <item>200</item>
     <item>300</item>
     <item>300</item>
     <item>300</item>
     <item>300</item>
     <item>400</item>
     <item>400</item>
     <item>400</item>
     <item>400</item>
     <item>500</item>
     <item>500</item>
     <item>500</item>
     <item>500</item>

   </integer-array>

</resources>
```

2. You parse through this file with the same technique you used before. The first
    list of items is the x coordinate; the y coordinate is found in the second list. You
    create each sprite by pairing the first entry from the x list with the first entry
    from the y list and then move down until you've created every block. Notice
    that you must type the total number of blocks at the top of the XML file—in
    this case, you have 32 pieces of the pier.

3. This game requires a number of new sprite objects, integers, and arrays. You
    need to add those to the top of the GameView class before you implement them.
    Listing 8-2 contains the new declarations; place them at the top of the file.

Listing 8-2. Initializing the Objects/Variables for Your Project

```
//SpriteObjects
private SpriteObject[] pier;
private SpriteObject[] cannon;
private SpriteObject ground;
private SpriteObject castle;
private SpriteObject[] boat;

//Variables
private Resources res;
```

```
private int[] x_coords;
private int[] y_coords;
private int boat_count = 0;
private int cannon_count = 3;
private int pier_count;
```

4. Although these sprites and integers look similar to those you've created before, it's important to notice that boat_count is set to 0. This lets you start the game without any boats and add them as you go. Also, you set cannon_count to 3 because originally you only deal with three cannons.

5. Add the code in Listing 8-3 to the GameView constructor. This code should look very much like the TabletPaddle code; they're identical except for the name of the object you're creating. Then, in the onDraw() function, you cycle through each pier and draw it onto the screen.

Listing 8-3. Creating the Pier

```
//pier sprites
pier_count = res.getInteger(R.integer.blocknumber);
x_coords = res.getIntArray(R.array.x);
y_coords = res.getIntArray(R.array.y);
pier = new SpriteObject[pier_count];
for(int i = 0; i < pier_count; i++){
        pier[i] = new SpriteObject(BitmapFactory.decodeResource(getResources(),
R.drawable.pier), x_coords[i], y_coords[i]);
}
```

6. Put the code in Listing 8-4 into the onDraw() method of GameView.

Listing 8-4. Drawing the Pier

```
for(int i = 0; i < pier_count; i++){
        pier[i].draw(canvas);
}
```

Because pier blocks don't need to do anything, you don't need to create code for them in the update() function. Let's move on to the ground and castle.

Adding the Ground and Castle

The ground and castle are more inanimate objects. You take care of them just as you took care of the piers. Luckily, there is only one of each, which means you don't need to use more XML data:

1. Listing 8-5 shows the code you use in the GameView constructor for the two sprites. Add it now.

Listing 8-5. Creating the Ground and Castle

```
ground = new SpriteObject(BitmapFactory.decodeResource(getResources(), R.drawable.ground),
480, 500);
```

```
castle = new SpriteObject(BitmapFactory.decodeResource(getResources(), R.drawable.castle),
890, 500);
```

2.   The trick with these two sprites is to make sure they're both in the right place. The order in which they're drawn is also important. Figure 8-2 shows what happens when the onDraw() function is called. You can see the layers of the images being drawn.

Figure 8-2. Image layers

3.   The ground must be below the pier and above the blue background. Likewise, the castle must be on top of the ground. To get the sequence right, Listing 8-6 contains a new onDraw() routine. Be sure the order is right: if the ground appears above the castle, then you would have a subterranean fortress that doesn't work so well in the game!

Listing 8-6. Drawing the Castle and Ground

```
canvas.drawColor(Color.BLUE);
ground.draw(canvas);
castle.draw(canvas);

for(int i = 0; i < pier_count; i++){
        pier[i].draw(canvas);
}
```

The next sprite objects you create will be added after the pier pieces are drawn. This makes sense because the cannons must be on top of the piers; the boats glide along the water and possibly hit the castle.

Creating the Boats

The boats are the most complicated sprites you must deal with. The user has no control over them, so their movement must be preprogrammed to follow a specific route. Adding some complexity, you must change the image of the sprite based on its direction. This all comes together in the update() function. For now, though, you can create an array to hold the boats without actually making them:

1.   Put the snippet from Listing 8-7 into your GameView constructor method.

Listing 8-7. Creating 12 Boat Sprites

```
//boat sprites
boat = new SpriteObject[12];
```

2.   Listing 8-8 shows the routine that cycles through the drawing of the available boats. Put this code in the onDraw() function after the other sprites are drawn.

Listing 8-8. Drawing the Boats

```
for(int i = 0; i < boat_count; i++){
        boat[i].draw(canvas);
}
```

3. The exciting part is coming up. Before you move forward, you need to understand the boat_count variable. Back in the GameView variable declarations, you initialized this integer by setting it equal to 0. So, in the original state, no boat sprites are drawn, because i isn't less than boat_count. You can picture boat_count as a collection of the available boats.

4. Because you start with no boats, the method for their creation is a bit more involved. Listing 8-9 contains the code you need to add to the update() function. I break it into its critical parts afterward. To make it work, import java.util,Random at the top of GameView.java.

Listing 8-9. Creating Boats and Random Intervals

```
Random random_boat = new Random();
int check_boat = random_boat.nextInt(100);

if(check_boat > 97 && boat_count < 12){
        int previous_boat = boat_count - 1;
        if(boat_count == 0 || boat[previous_boat].getX() > 150){
                boat[boat_count] = new
SpriteObject(BitmapFactory.decodeResource(getResources(), R.drawable.boat), 100, 150);
                boat[boat_count].setMoveX(3);
                boat_count++;
        }
}
```

5. First, you make a random number generator. You call a nextInt() method that selects an integer between 0 and the argument. The check_boat variable is tested so that you create boats at random intervals.

⬛ **Note** Creating a random number generator and getting an integer between zero and your own value is a perfect way to add some randomness to your games. You no longer have to worry about a decimal number because integers are much easier to work with. Remember to run your games many times in tests if you use random elements because you may find unexpected behavior if the random numbers are different than the ones you expected.

---

6. The first if statement proceeds only if the random number is greater than 97, which is very unlikely but keeps the onslaught of boats to a minimum. Then you require that boat_count be less than 12. This prevents many boats from being on the field at the same time. If this proves to be too easy for the player, you can increase this number and make the game much more challenging.

7. The second if statement checks to see if the new boat would be the first boat or if it's a certain distance from the previous boat. You do this by incrementing boat_count back by 1 and testing to see if the x coordinates of the prior boat are more than 150. Otherwise, the boats could appear on top of each other, which detracts from the appearance of the game (although it could make the game more challenging!).

8. If the boat passes all the if statements, then it's initialized with a starting x position of 100. You move it at the rather slow pace of three pixels per update() function. Here is another great opportunity to add difficulty by slowly increasing the speed of the boats when the player reaches a certain score or other achievement.

9. Finally, boat_count is incremented to let the draw() functions handle the newly added boat. Your fleet has expanded.

10. You need to change the direction of the boats so they can make the appropriate turn to head toward their destination: the castle. The code in Listing 8-10 does this; add it to the update() method.

Listing 8-10. Changing the Boat Direction

```
for(int i = 0; i < boat_count; i++){
        if((int)boat[i].getX() > 950){
                boat[i].setMoveX(0);
                boat[i].setMoveY(3);
                boat[i].setBitmap(BitmapFactory.decodeResource(getResources(),
R.drawable.boatdown));
        }
}
```

11. When the boat gets to the x location of 950 pixels, it stops moving to the right and begins its descent. Notice the final line: you change the sprite image because ships rarely move without changing orientation. To do this, rotate the original boat image 90 degrees and save it as a new resource called boatdown.

That's it. When you add the cannon, you see ships randomly appear and head toward your castle.

Adding Cannons

As is true for the boats, the number of cannons changes during the game. For now, you're only worried about proving the concept. Follow these steps:

1. Put the code in Listing 8-11 into the GameView creator. You can change the value of cannon_count in its declaration to create even more cannons. Instead of responding to user input, you make the cannons appear on three consecutive pier blocks with a quick loop that move the cannons 100 units each time.

Listing 8-11. Changing the Value of Cannon Count

```
//cannon sprites
cannon = new SpriteObject[cannon_count];
for(int i = 0; i < cannon_count; i++){
        cannon[i] = new SpriteObject(BitmapFactory.decodeResource(getResources(),
R.drawable.cannonup), (580 + i * 100), 200);
}
```

2. To ready yourself to create additional cannon sprites, name the original drawing cannonup. This will make it easier when the user wishes to change the cannon's orientation.

3. Add the code from Listing 8-12 to the onDraw() function, and your cannonry will appear when the game runs.

Listing 8-12. Drawing the Cannons

```
for(int i = 0; i < cannon_count; i++){
        cannon[i].draw(canvas);
}
```

You have some simple remaining issues to handle. The framework of the game is finished.

Adding Images

The images I used are available at http://code.google.com/p/android-tablet-games/, or you can make your own creations. Figures 8-3 through 8-7 show the images I used to build Harbor Defender; their dimensions are specified in the figure captions. Later, I make some suggestions about how to create your images. Remember that sometimes you need to rotate or flip them to display them in an alternate state.

Figure 8-3. Castle: 200 × 100

Figure 8-4. Boat and boatdown: 50 × 30 and 30 × 50, respectively

Figure 8-5. Ground: 800 × 250

Figure 8-6. `Pier: 100 × 100`

Figure 8-7. Cannon: 100 × 100

Debugging Harbor Defender

With a simple approach to how the game looks, you're ready to try it. Load it as you would any game, and you see boats slowly appear and cruise down toward the castle. If you wait long enough, they pass through the castle and off the screen.

If things don't work this way, or you get an error like the one displayed in Figure 8-8, or the game closes at startup, then you have some work to do. This section is dedicated to fixing common problems in game development for Android. It doesn't go into specific problems because there is no way to anticipate every error. It should be fairly obvious how to fix errors in your code if Eclipse catches them, but the runtime issues can be more difficult.

Here is the process to use:

1. Make sure you're using LogCat to get information on the emulator. This is critical when you use Log.d in your program to alert you when certain events are triggered. LogCat also displays fairly detailed reports about errors.

147

2. Don't close the emulator when you get an error. Look at the issue in Figure 8-2. You may be tempted to close out immediately, but doing so erases the LogCat results. Instead, wait so you can diagnose the problem.

Figure 8-8. Runtime error in Harbor Defender

3. Scroll up the LogCat readout, shown in Figure 8-9, and you should find phrases in a red font that signal where the error occurred. Luckily, the error notes the exact line numbers that were the problem.

Log				
Time		pid	tag	Message
08-24 03:50:20.019	V	371	dalvikvm	threadid=11 thread exiting with uncaught exception (group=0x4001
08-24 03:50:20.019	E	371	AndroidRuntime	FATAL EXCEPTION Thread-11
08-24 03:50:20.019	E	371	AndroidRuntime	java.lang.NullPointerException
08-24 03:50:20.019	E	371	AndroidRuntime	at com.gameproject.harbordefender.GameView.onDraw(GameView.ja
08-24 03:50:20.019	E	371	AndroidRuntime	at com.gameproject.harbordefender.GameLogic.run(GameLogic.jav
08-24 03:50:20.079	V	75	ActivityManager	Force finishing activity com.gameproject.harbordefender.MainAc
08-24 03:50:20.119	V	75	WindowManager	Failure taking screenshot for (216x135) to layer 21020

Figure 8-9. LogCat NullPointerException

4. You only need to pay attention to the earlier error lines in most cases. In this case, the onDraw() function failed when the cannons were being drawn. The reason is that I commented out the initialization of the cannon sprites. This is a common problem when you're dealing with a game that has sprites being created and destroyed. Make sure all the sprites you reference for drawing or updating actually exist.

5. A final suggestion for working with errors is to make your emulator smaller. If you have a relatively small screen size, then your emulator may take up most of the screen. This prevents you from looking at the LogCat while you're working. To fix this, choose Run   Run_configuration. Then go to the Target tab and scroll down. In the command-line options, type in **scale .8**. This shrinks the emulator to 80% of its original size.

▪ **Note** If your best efforts to fix a problem don't succeed, try searching for a solution on StackOverFlow (http://stackoverflow.com/). In the future, though, make small changes between tests. This way, you can go back to the previous state that worked. Be ready to always come back to something that you know worked.

The next chapter involves many different fixes and updates to the game. Most notably, you enable the user to move and rotate cannons. In your previous games, the player has never had this many options, and it will be a unique exercise.

Another addition is a point system that rewards the player for each boat that is destroyed. The physics must also be updated because you need to end the game once a boat strikes the castle rather than having the boat pass right through.

You also have to worry about a new factor: inappropriate user interaction. It makes sense for the user to click a piece of the pier to put a cannon onto it, but what if they miss the pier and click the ocean? This requires you to evaluate each input quickly and efficiently to respond immediately to the user, yet also prevent cannons from appearing where they don't belong.

To finalize your work, you add input and logic to polish the overall appearance of the game.

Summary

You've gone through the process of setting up a real game. With the elements in place, you're ready to add the features that make the game a fun user experience. You should be comfortable planning a game and organizing the way to handle the sprites and objects that make it up.

As you look to the future, you'll focus more on the player experience rather than on the limits of your technical abilities. Creating the artwork for a game is often a limiting factor as well, but a fun and creative game can make up for many shortcomings. For now, let's get your game ready for deployment.

CHAPTER 9

A One-Player Strategy Game

Part 2: Coding the Game

With the framework in place, you can now write the code to create a playable game. The trick here is always to make your code as efficient as possible. When games become more complex and involve more sprites, they can begin to slow as the processor struggles to keep up. You avoid this with some clever techniques that can ease the load.

Keeping the end goal in mind as you progress is also critical because you must have a functioning game before you can add the bells and whistles that differentiate your work from others. In fact, in my experience, knowing when to stop working on a game and release it is always the trickiest part. There is a fine line between a game that is too simple and a game that is unplayable because it's overloaded with features and additions that a normal user doesn't have time to learn.

Note As you progress through the code in this chapter, recall that putting Log.d statements into the code can help clarify what is happening and which functions are being called. Some of the code can be quite complex, and I still use this technique to help me step through the methods, especially if I'm not getting the desired behavior.

Here is a list of the features you must complete in this chapter in order to have a working game:

- Enhancing the sprite objects
- Shooting bullets out of the cannons
- Eliminating boats after they have been hit
- Restarting the game when boats hit the castle

Some of these—like lowering the health of a boat when a bullet hits it—are easily completed, but others require some thought and clever coding. To simplify your editing, I've posted the entire methods for this chapter. This way, you can ensure that your previous work is exactly what is needed for the final game. This also helps you see how each function calls the others and what information is shared among them.

The next section begins with our improvements to SpriteObject.java. You make very few modifications, but the changes that you do make will simplify your work in GameView.java.

Enhancing the Game Sprites

In this game, you demand a lot from your sprites. To handle the new functionality, you need a couple of new methods and variables that all the sprites use. Although only one sprite may actually take advantage of a particular feature, rather than create additional classes, you have every game sprite inherit from SpriteObject because the sprites are largely the same—there is no need to clutter the project.

However, if you expand the game, and you want the boats to be able to fire back, change direction, or spawn smaller boats, then you might want to create a special boat class that embodies these capabilities. Any time a sprite or object uses two or more unique functions, I usually make a new class for it.

Follow these steps to modify SpriteObject.java:

1. Listing 9-1 shows the new variables to add and the values you assign them. Add this code at the top of SpriteObject.java.

Listing 9-1. SpriteObject Variables

```
private int health = 3;
private int Orientation = -1;
public int LEFT = 0;
public int RIGHT = 1;
public int UP = 2;
public int DOWN = 3;
private boolean stack = false;
```

2. The use of the variables in Listing 9-1 is apparent in the functions shown in Listing 9-2. Type all of this code at the end of SpriteObject. The new methods are used liberally by your sprites.

Listing 9-2. New Functions for SpriteObject

```
public boolean cursor_selection(int cursor_x, int cursor_y){

        int sprite_right = (int)(getBitmap().getWidth() + getX());
        int sprite_bottom = (int)(getBitmap().getHeight() + getY());
        if(cursor_x > getX() && cursor_x < sprite_right && cursor_y > getY() && cursor_y <
sprite_bottom){
                return true;
        }
        else{
                return false;
        }

}

public void setStacked(boolean s){
        stack = s;
}
public boolean getStacked(){
        return stack;
}
```

```
public void diminishHealth(int m){
        health -= m;
}
public int getHealth(){
        return health;
}
public void setOrientation(int o){
        Orientation = o;
}
public int getOrientation(){
        return Orientation;
}
```

The cursor_selection() function is a very powerful method that returns true if the user touches a sprite and remains false if they don't. It's basically a simple version of the collide() method, but it only worries about the input the user gives. You implement it in the way the user selects the type of cannon to add.

The functions related to whether the sprite is stacked are used to determine whether a piece of the pier already has a cannon on it. If a cannon exists there, you prevent the user from placing another one on top of it. Some spots are better locations than others, so it's unfair for the user to be able to layer cannons.

You add two functions to handle a sprite's health. The only sprite that has health in your game is the boats. When they have been hit three times, they're removed from the game.

3. You need to modify the SpriteObject update() function to check whether a sprite has lost all of its health. Replace the existing code with that in Listing 9-3.

Listing 9-3. Changing the update() Method

```
public void update(int adj_mov) {
        if(state == ALIVE){
                x += x_move;
                y += y_move;
                if(health <= 0){
                        state = DEAD;
                }
        }
}
```

The final addition checks which way a sprite is facing. You use this for the cannons. If a cannon faces down, for example, you must launch the bullet toward the bottom of the screen, whereas a cannon pointing right should send the bullet toward the right side of the screen.

Let's put these functions into action!

Creating the User Controls

The constructor method of GameView.java has several newcomers. This section dissects the new sprites that are used primarily for user interaction and also shows you a new concept. Rather than create four different cannon icons that point in all of the cardinal directions, you rotate one image for the four different sprites. This saves space on your machine, but it also causes some extra processor work at startup.

To demonstrate the alternative, the main cannons are all individual sprites that don't need to be rotated. The method you use on such occasions depends on your resources and how much space you have on disk.

Follow these steps:

1. Before you can start working with the new sprites, you must first declare the objects before your constructor. Put the code in Listing 9-4 inside GameView.java.

Listing 9-4. SpriteObjects for Harbor Defender

```java
private SpriteObject trash;
private SpriteObject dock;
private SpriteObject marker;
private SpriteObject cannonrightsmall;
private SpriteObject cannonleftsmall;
private SpriteObject cannonupsmall;
private SpriteObject cannondownsmall;
```

2. In the GameView constructor, initialize the trash, dock, and marker icons as shown in Listing 9-5. These three sprites create the foundation of your user controls. At lower right onscreen, a dock that holds the options. At the front of the dock is the trashcan that lets users destroy cannons they've built. The marker sprite jumps around behind the icons to show the player which one is currently selected.

Listing 9-5. Setting Up the Icons

```java
trash = new SpriteObject(BitmapFactory.decodeResource(getResources(), R.drawable.trash), 50,
650);
dock = new SpriteObject(BitmapFactory.decodeResource(getResources(), R.drawable.dock), 0,
650);
marker = new SpriteObject(BitmapFactory.decodeResource(getResources(), R.drawable.marker), 50,
650);
```

3. The next stage is creating the small cannon icons. Add the code shown in Listing 9-6 to the GameView constructor. This serves as the basis for your dock.

Listing 9-6. Making Miniature Cannon Icons

```java
Bitmap bcannonupsmall = BitmapFactory.decodeResource(getResources(),
R.drawable.cannonupsmall);
int w = bcannonupsmall.getWidth();
int h = bcannonupsmall.getHeight();
Matrix mtx = new Matrix();
mtx.postRotate(90);

Bitmap bcannonrightsmall = Bitmap.createBitmap(bcannonupsmall, 0, 0, h, w, mtx, true);
Bitmap bcannondownsmall = Bitmap.createBitmap(bcannonrightsmall, 0, 0, w, h, mtx, true);
Bitmap bcannonleftsmall = Bitmap.createBitmap(bcannondownsmall, 0, 0 , h, w, mtx, true);

cannonrightsmall = new SpriteObject(bcannonrightsmall, 110, 650);
```

```
cannonleftsmall = new SpriteObject(bcannonleftsmall, 180, 650);
cannondownsmall = new SpriteObject(bcannondownsmall, 240, 650);
cannonupsmall = new SpriteObject(bcannonupsmall, 300, 650);
```

If you think this code looks a little like Greek, don't worry. You create the miniature cannon-up sprite and gather its height and width. Then you initiate a new matrix that you rotate 90 degrees. Three new bitmaps are created by rotating cannondownsmall three times. The sprites are then created with the new images. The locations are very specific, to put all the icons on the small dock at lower left onscreen.

4. To make the dock useful, you need to store the user's selection with variables (in other words, if the user selects the cannon facing down, you need to know to create that type of cannon). You achieve this by putting the variables from Listing 9-7 at the top of GameView. User_choice stores the user's selection.

Listing 9-7. Variables to Store the User's Selections

```
Private int TRASH = 1;
Private int CANNON_LEFT = 2;
Private int CANNON_RIGHT = 3;
Private int CANNON_UP = 4;
Private int CANNON_DOWN = 5;
Private int user_choice;
```

5. You've created a nice dock with several options for the user to choose from, but you need to track where the user is pointing. You use four variables in referencing the user's selection. Add the variables from Listing 9-8 to the top of GameView.java.

Listing 9-8. Gathering Data About the Location of the Last Touch Event

```
private int cursor_x;
private int cursor_y;
private boolean selection_changed;
private boolean addboat;
```

6. Edit ProcessMotionEvent() to look like the code shown in Listing 9-9. This incorporates the first three of the variables you declared in step 5.

Listing 9-9. Storing the User's Input

```
public void processMotionEvent(InputObject input){
        selection_changed = true;
        cursor_x = input.x;
        cursor_y = input.y;

}
```

With this code in place, when a touch occurs on the tablet, you set selection_changed to true and store the location of the touch with the variables cursor_x and cursor_y.

7. In the update() function, you use the data from step 6 to determine whether you need to handle a user-input event and where the user is interacting. Add

the code in Listing 9-10 to the update() method of GameView.java. This is how you handle the user input.

Listing 9-10. Handling User Input in the update() Function

```
if(selection_changed){
        selection_changed = false;
        if(trash.cursor_selection(cursor_x, cursor_y)){
                user_choice = TRASH;
                marker.setX(50);
                addboat = false;
        }
        if(cannonrightsmall.cursor_selection(cursor_x, cursor_y)){
                user_choice = CANNON_RIGHT;
                marker.setX(110);
                addboat = true;
        }
        if(cannonleftsmall.cursor_selection(cursor_x, cursor_y)){
                user_choice = CANNON_LEFT;
                marker.setX(180);
                addboat = true;
        }
        if(cannondownsmall.cursor_selection(cursor_x, cursor_y)){
                user_choice = CANNON_DOWN;
                marker.setX(240);
                addboat = true;
        }
        if(cannonupsmall.cursor_selection(cursor_x, cursor_y)){
                user_choice = CANNON_UP;
                marker.setX(300);
                addboat = true;
        }
        else if(addboat){
                if(cannon_count < 10){
                        for(int i = 0; i < pier_count; i++){
                                if(pier[i].cursor_selection(cursor_x, cursor_y)){
                                        if(pier[i].getStacked() == false){
                                                switch(user_choice){
                                                case 2:
                                                        cannon[cannon_count] = new
SpriteObject(BitmapFactory.decodeResource(getResources(), R.drawable.cannonleft),
(int)pier[i].getX(), (int)pier[i].getY());

cannon[cannon_count].setOrientation(cannon[cannon_count].LEFT);
                                                        break;

                                                case 3:
                                                        cannon[cannon_count] = new
SpriteObject(BitmapFactory.decodeResource(getResources(), R.drawable.cannonright),
(int)pier[i].getX(), (int)pier[i].getY());

cannon[cannon_count].setOrientation(cannon[cannon_count].RIGHT);
```

```
                                             break;

                             case 4:
                                   cannon[cannon_count] = new
SpriteObject(BitmapFactory.decodeResource(getResources(), R.drawable.cannonup),
(int)pier[i].getX(), (int)pier[i].getY());

cannon[cannon_count].setOrientation(cannon[cannon_count].UP);
                                             break;

                             case 5:
                                   cannon[cannon_count] = new
SpriteObject(BitmapFactory.decodeResource(getResources(), R.drawable.cannondown),
(int)pier[i].getX(), (int)pier[i].getY());

cannon[cannon_count].setOrientation(cannon[cannon_count].DOWN);
                                             break;
                                   }

                                   cannon_count++;
                                   pier[i].setStacked(true);
                             }
                             else if(pier[i].getStacked() == true){
                                   if(user_choice == 1){
                                         for(int u = 0; u < cannon_count; u++){
                                               if(cannon[u].getX() ==
pier[i].getX() && cannon[u].getY() == pier[i].getY()){

cannon[u].setstate(cannon[u].DEAD);
                                                     }
                                               }
                                         }
                                   }
                             }
                       }
                 }
           }
     }
}
```

This code deals with the dock icons. The other side of the user interaction is the actual placing of the boats onscreen. When the player selects any of the boats or the trashcan, they set addboat to true. This means you need to look for what the user is doing with the game. The variable user_choice stores the last dock icon that the user selected.

The processor cycles through the pier pieces; it stops when it finds that the user has touched a pier block. It then asks whether the pier is stacked. You saw earlier that being *stacked* in this case means the pier is already holding a cannon. If it isn't, then the user is free to add a cannon to that pier. The code then goes into a switch statement.

The numbers for the cases of the switch correspond to the variables you assigned in the constructor method (for example, whether the cannon is pointing to the left). When you find the orientation of the cannon that the player desires, you create the new sprite, using the location of the pier. It's very important that your pier and cannons occupy the same area (100 × 100). This makes positioning a simple matter.

Placing cannons isn't the only thing players can do, however. They can also select the trashcan, which has a value of 1. The trash performs in the opposite fashion from what you saw previously: it looks for a pier block that is stacked, finds the cannon that is placed there, and removes it.

That's it. The user can now control your game. The next sections add features to your bullets and boats.

Putting Everything on the Screen

Now that you have lots of great features like your user interface controls and boats, you need to add them to the screen. To do so, the onDraw() function needs an adjustment. Listing 9-11 contains the entire code for the function.

Ensure that your onDraw function looks exactly like Listing 9-11 or the images will not be drawn to the screen.

Listing 9-11. onDraw()

```
@Override
public void onDraw(Canvas canvas) {
        canvas.drawColor(Color.BLUE);
        ground.draw(canvas);

        //the user controls
        dock.draw(canvas);
        marker.draw(canvas);
        trash.draw(canvas);
        cannonleftsmall.draw(canvas);
        cannonrightsmall.draw(canvas);
        cannondownsmall.draw(canvas);
        cannonupsmall.draw(canvas);


        for(int i = 0; i < pier_count; i++){
                pier[i].draw(canvas);
        }
        for(int i = 0; i < boat_count; i++){
                boat[i].draw(canvas);
        }
        for(int i = 0; i < cannon_count; i++){
                cannon[i].draw(canvas);
        }
        for(int i = 0; i < 50; i++){
                bullets[i].draw(canvas);
        }
        castle.draw(canvas);
}
```

Check out the group of sprites under the heading "user controls." These include the dock, the marker, and the trash and cannon icons that users can select. The important note here is that the dock is obviously drawn first, then the marker, and then the icons. This way, you can always see the dock in the background. The marker is then free to highlight all of the icons from behind. Figure 9-1 shows how the dock looks.

Figure 9-1. The dock containing the user controls that the user can interact with

At the end of the function, four for loops go through the lists of sprites. Finally, the castle is drawn. You always draw every bullet, even though they may or may not be moving at the current time. This is taken care of by the SpriteObject class when it checks to ensure that sprites are alive before drawing them. With bullets ready to destroy the boats, we must create and keep track of the oncoming enemies. The next section covers the ins and outs of handling the boats.

Deploying and Managing the Attack Boats

Listing 9-12 contains code for the entire GameView.java update() method that deals with the boats. . If you don't understand a portion of it, type it in its entirety and run the game. You can see how it works based on the game's behavior.

1. Make sure that your update() method includes all of the code here. After the listing, you will find a explanation of it.

Listing 9-12. Setting Up the Boats in the update() Function

```
public void update(int adj_mov) {

        for(int i = 0; i < boat_count; i++){
                if((int)boat[i].getX() > 950){
                        boat[i].setMoveX(0);
                        boat[i].setMoveY(3);
                        boat[i].setBitmap(BitmapFactory.decodeResource(getResources(),
R.drawable.boatdown));
                }
        }

        Random random_boat = new Random();
        int check_boat = random_boat.nextInt(100);

        if(check_boat > 97 && boat_count < 12){
                int previous_boat = boat_count - 1;
                if(boat_count == 0 || boat[previous_boat].getX() > 150){
                        boat[boat_count] = new
SpriteObject(BitmapFactory.decodeResource(getResources(), R.drawable.boat), 100, 150);
                        boat[boat_count].setMoveX(3);
                        boat_count++;
                }
        }
}
```

The code from Listing 9-12 was completed in Chapter 8.. The first `for` loop determines whether the boat has moved to the right too much. If it has, then a new sprite image is used, and it begins to travel down the screen toward the castle.

The next block handles the creation of random boats. The most important portion is where you use an `if` statement to ensure that the previous boat is adequately separated from the new boat. Again, you increment the number of boats and set the new craft on its way, as shown in Listing 9-12.

Now we will check for a collision with the castle which would result in a loss for the player.

2. Add the for-loop in Listing 9-13 in your update() method.

Listing 9-13. Testing for a Collision with the Castle, and Resetting the Game

```
for(int i = 0; i < boat_count; i++){
        if(boat[i].collide(castle)){
                reset();
        }
}
```

If the user fails and the boat strikes the castle, then you call a new function called `reset()`. You look at what this simple function does in a bit. (I could have included all of the code here, but I find it easier visually to add extra functions to handle distinct tasks.)

With boats sailing and bullets ready to fire, we need to work on our cannons. You cannot defeat the boats without them. Check out the next section that handles the way we manipulate and use cannons.

Firing the Cannons

After the user input, the bullets are the most complex portion of the game. Keeping track of 50 sprites that can move in four different directions and may or may not be alive at the current moment is tricky. The cannons are about to get a lot more exciting. In this section, you add the bullets and write the code that handles how and when the cannons fire their volleys of shots.

Follow these steps:

1. Add the code in Listing 9-14 to the `GameView` constructor. This code handles the new bullets the cannons shoot. The number of bullets onscreen is limited to 50 to keep things simple. There are two arrays: one contains the bullet sprites (`bullets[]`) and the other holding the list of bullets that aren't currently in use (`available_bullet[]`).

Listing 9-14. Additions to the onCreate() method that handle the bullets.

```
available_bullet = new int[50];
for(int i = 0; i < 50; i++){
        available_bullet[i] = i;
}

bullets = new SpriteObject[50];
for(int i = 0; i < 50; i++){
        bullets[i] = new SpriteObject(BitmapFactory.decodeResource(getResources(),
R.drawable.bullet), 10, 10);
        bullets[i].setState(bullets[i].DEAD);
}
```

You declare an array of integers in which every bullet is available, because you know that none have been fired yet. The bullets sprites are initialized as well. You set their state to DEAD because you don't want bullets to appear without having been fired.

    2.   Add the code in Listing 9-15 to the update() method. First, you set the available_bullet array equal to zero; this will make calculations easier as you go along. Then you create a very important variable: g = 0. g is used to specify which bullets are available and which aren't.

Listing 9-15. Resetting the List of Available Bullets

```
for(int f = 0; f < 50; f++){
        available_bullet[f] = 0;
}

int g = 0;
```

    3.   Immediately after clearing the array, place the code from Listing 9-16 into the update() method.

Listing 9-16. Handling Changes in Bullets

```
for(int i = 0; i < 50; i++){

if(bullets[i].getY() > 800 || bullets[i].getX() > 1280 || bullets[i].getY() < 0 ||
bullets[i].getX() < 0){
                bullets[i].setstate(bullets[i].DEAD);
        }

        for(int b = 0; b < boat_count; b++){
                if(bullets[i].collide(boat[b])){
                        boat[b].diminishHealth(1);
                        bullets[i].setstate(bullets[i].DEAD);
                }
        }
}

bullets[i].update(adj_mov);
```

```
        if(bullets[i].getstate() == bullets[i].DEAD){
                available_bullet[g] = i;
                g++;
        }

}
```

A loop goes through every bullet sprite. The first if statement checks to see if the bullet has left the screen; if it has, you set its state to DEAD. This means it can be reused as an available bullet in your next iteration. A for loop handles boat collisions. If the boat is hit, then its health goes down by one, and you destroy the bullet. Again, the bullet can now be reused. A simple update() call changes the location of the bullet based on its moveX and moveY.

If the bullet is dead, then you list it as an available bullet. If you look closely at the if statement, you notice that the first dead bullet is given the first spot in the available_bullet array, g is incremented, and the next dead bullet is given the next slot.

4. With the bullets ready to go, it's time to worry about the firing mechanism. Fifty iterations of the update() function release a bullet from every cannon on the playing field. The code in Listing 9-17 performs these with a call to the new function createBullet(), which takes four arguments. Put this code into the update() method immediately after the code you've already added to the method.

Listing 9-17. Calculating When to Fire a Volley of Bullets

```
shooting_counter++;
if(shooting_counter >= 50){
        shooting_counter = 0;
        int round = 0;
        for(int i = 0; i < cannon_count; i++){
                if(cannon[i].getOrientation() == cannon[i].LEFT){
                        int x = (int)(cannon[i].getX());
                        int y = (int)(cannon[i].getY() + cannon[i].getBitmap().getHeight()/2);
                        createBullet(x,y,cannon[i].LEFT, round);
                        round++;
                }
                if(cannon[i].getOrientation() == cannon[i].RIGHT){
                        int x = (int)(cannon[i].getX() + cannon[i].getBitmap().getWidth());
                        int y = (int)(cannon[i].getY() + cannon[i].getBitmap().getHeight()/2);
                        createBullet(x,y,cannon[i].RIGHT, round);
                        round++;
                }
                if(cannon[i].getOrientation() == cannon[i].UP){
                        int x = (int)(cannon[i].getX() + cannon[i].getBitmap().getWidth()/2);
                        int y = (int)(cannon[i].getY());
                        createBullet(x,y,cannon[i].UP, round);
                        round++;
                }
        if(cannon[i].getOrientation() == cannon[i].DOWN){
                        int x = (int)(cannon[i].getX() + cannon[i].getBitmap().getWidth()/2);
                        int y = (int)(cannon[i].getY() + cannon[i].getBitmap().getHeight());
                        createBullet(x,y,cannon[i].DOWN, round);
```

```
                        round++;
                }
        }
}
```

This block of code creates the variable round, which tracks which bullet has been fired. The first cannon fires round one, the second cannon fires round two, and so on. The series of if statements uses the new getOrientation() function you created in SpriteObject.java. The x and y coordinates of the end of the barrel of each cannon are then passed to the createBullet() method. Getting the coordinates requires some calculations because you know the barrel is in the center of the cannon.

The mechanics of the bullets make even more sense in createBullet(), which you'll write in the next section; the code in Listing 9-17 simply sends the necessary information to that method. Because you've initialized all the bullet sprites already, this doesn't waste processing because you're only updating the sprites.

5. To finish the update() method, make sure you have the calls to the various sprites' update() functions as shown in Listing 9-18.

Listing 9-18. Including the Basic update() Functions

```
castle.update(adj_mov);
ground.update(adj_mov);
for(int i = 0; i < boat_count; i++){
        boat[i].update(adj_mov);
}

}
```

The next section ties up the loose ends by handling game resets and firing bullets.

Managing Game Outcomes

When the player loses the game and a boat hits the castle, you call reset(). This is a simple and quick function.

Follow these steps:

1. Add the code from Listing 9-19 below the other functions in GameView.

Listing 9-19. reset() Method

```
private void reset(){
        for(int i = 0; i < boat_count; i++){
                boat[i].setstate(boat[i].DEAD);
        }
        boat_count = 0;

}
```

All you do is destroy the boats. This, in effect, restarts the game, because the boats are randomly created once again. You don't remove the cannons because there is no need to worry about them. The user can delete them if they wish. If you want to display a message to the user, you can create a sprite and draw it onscreen at this point. In the update() function, have it wait for 30 or so cycles, and then remove the message.

2. The createBullet() method is a bit more involved, as you can see in Listing 9-20, but it's definitely manageable. Put this method directly below the reset() function.

Listing 9-20. createBullet() Method

```
private void createBullet(int x, int y, int direction, int r){
        if(r >= 0){
                int index = available_bullet[r];
                if(direction == bullets[index].RIGHT){
                        bullets[index].setMoveX(10);
                        bullets[index].setMoveY(0);
                        bullets[index].setX(x);
                        bullets[index].setY(y);
                        bullets[index].setstate(bullets[index].ALIVE);
                }
                if(direction == bullets[index].LEFT){
                        bullets[index].setMoveX(-10);
                        bullets[index].setMoveY(0);
                        bullets[index].setX(x);
                        bullets[index].setY(y);
                        bullets[index].setstate(bullets[index].ALIVE);
                }
                if(direction == bullets[index].UP){
                        bullets[index].setMoveY(-10);
                        bullets[index].setMoveX(0);
                        bullets[index].setX(x);
                        bullets[index].setY(y);
                        bullets[index].setstate(bullets[index].ALIVE);
                }
                if(direction == bullets[index].DOWN){
                        bullets[index].setMoveY(10);
                        bullets[index].setMoveX(0);
                        bullets[index].setX(x);
                        bullets[index].setY(y);
                        bullets[index].setstate(bullets[index].ALIVE);
                }
        }
}
```

The bullet sprites are symmetrical, so you don't have to worry about their orientation, only the direction of their movement. Don't forget the last line of each if block, which makes the bullets alive. Otherwise, they will never be drawn, and you'll have trouble figuring out what went wrong.

You've finally finished the game project. The next section gives you some ideas for future plans.

Analyzing the Game

If you haven't already, run the game. When the boats start coming, place your cannons to defend the castle. I wish you luck in your battle.

Here is a list of features and techniques you've used to build Harbor Defender. Be proud of your incredible effort to persevere through the code, errors, and work:

- Game loop

- Multiple sprites

- Drawing images to the screen

- Bitmap manipulation

- User interaction

- Some AI

- Collision detection

- XML data parsing

- And much more

With an entire game written, you can relax and change the game into whatever you desire. If you make enough changes, maybe you can make some money off it in the Android Market. The final chapter of the book discusses this possibility.

Having an expandable game is critical. If game developers had to make each game from scratch, they would never release enough games to pay the rent. Instead, they transform frameworks into a number of unique and seemingly different creations. What you've done has the potential to be transformed into a maze game, a platform game, a turn-based strategy game, or many other possibilities.

The SpriteObject class is completely reusable, and GameView can fairly easily be adjusted into other types. If you need ideas, I find it fun to look through other game-development books and create their samples for Android. Any game for any language can probably be created on Android. This can be a challenge if the game was made for a computer and uses keyboard controls. Be creative, and I'm sure you can write some very different programs.

Figure 9-2 shows the completed game. See if you can envision its being transformed into a dozen different projects.

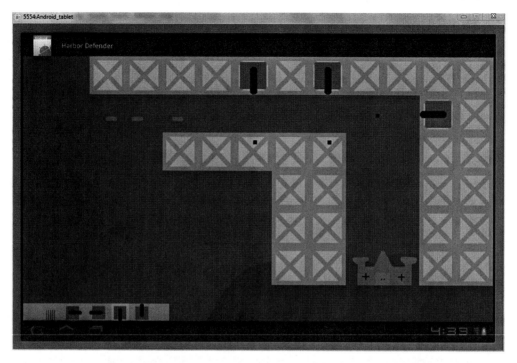

Figure 9-2. Your completed project

Summary

Your hard work is finished, and you've learned a lot. Most recently in this chapter, you saw how to use a matrix to rotate a bitmap. You also checked out how to keep track of 50 sprites and maintain another list of which sprites are dead and ready to be created again. This chapter also marked your first foray into creating a user interface that includes several icons and a marker to show the user what is currently selected.

If you're tired of code, there is great news: the next chapter deals with publishing your game, providing updates, and handling the business end. You look at what games sell well and how tablets are changing the computing landscape. When you understand the business aspects, it's your turn to create your own masterpiece!

CHAPTER 10

Publishing the Game

Your game is ready for the masses, but you have a couple more steps before the app can be consumed by the public. There are a couple of modifications to the code that you can use to polish your work. Then this chapter goes over the steps involved in selling your game or giving it away. Finally, you look at ways to ensure success in the competitive market for mobile apps.

Making a quality game is only the first step toward achieving best-seller status in the Android App Market. Everything you've done so far can be incorporated in how you present your final product. The graphics, sounds, and appearance of the app are integrated into how you sell it to consumers.

Polishing the Application

Although your game is playable as is, it could use some polishing. A welcome screen would be a nice addition so players can learn about the game before jumping into it. You have a lot of options when it comes to adding this feature, but making a rudimentary entrance screen is easy, and you can fine-tune it for each game. In this section, you add a screen and then a button to start up the game.

Adding an Splash Screen

Because GameView.java takes care of the actual game and its appearance, your startup page is handled by MainActivity.java. Instead of setting the screen to show GameView, you present a quick layout and then give the user the ability to enter the game. This makes your work more professional and easier for the user. To expand on this concept, you could play a short video clip to introduce the game, but I leave that to your imagination.

Take a look at Figure 10-1 to see what your splash screen looks like. This section discusses ways of adding features and items to it if you desire a more complete intro screen.

Figure 10-1. Introduction to your game

To achieve the look in Figure 10-1, let's go back to a concept explored in Chapter 1. The appearance of the app is generated in `main.xml`, where you can create the interface by dragging buttons and text onto the screen. You then edit the text and elements. The following steps show how to do this:

1. Find your main.xml file in the Harbor Defender project by navigating the folders: `res  layout  main.xml`.

2. Open `main.xml`, and select "10.1in WXGA (tablet)" from the drop-down menu near the top. The first order of business is to look at the code for the main.xml file.

3. Select `main.xml` on the small tab near the bottom of the screen.

4. Replace the existing code with the code in Listing 10-1.

Listing 10-1. `Main.xml`

```
<?xml version="1.0" encoding="utf-8"?>



<AbsoluteLayout
        xmlns:android="http://schemas.android.com/apk/res/android"
```

```
      android:orientation="vertical"
      android:layout_width="fill_parent"
      android:layout_height="fill_parent"
   >
```

`</AbsoluteLayout>`

You replace the existing LinearLayout with an AbsoluteLayout. Both of these are frameworks to which you can add layout elements. The AbsoluteLayout, however, lets you quickly specify the exact location for the elements, whereas the LinearLayout aligns all of the items toward the left. This is critical when you add the parts of your welcome screen.

5. Return to the graphical layout by selecting the small Graphical Layout tab at the bottom of the screen.

6. You use the palette of items on the left to create your layout. Figure 10-2 shows what this will look like. Drag a Button and a TextView onto your screen. They contain filler text for now, but you edit it shortly.

Figure 10-2. Using the palette on the left to drag the TextView and Button objects onto the screen

7. It's time to go back to the view of the code. Select the main.xml tab at the bottom of the screen. You should observe that two new elements (Button and TextView) have appeared in your AbsoluteLayout element.

8. You need to plug in your text and change the id of the button. Check out the bold code in Listing 10-2. You can use different words, but the important part is to remember the name or other identifier that you assign to the button's id.

Listing 10-2. `Main.xml`

```xml
<?xml version="1.0" encoding="utf-8"?>


<AbsoluteLayout
        xmlns:android="http://schemas.android.com/apk/res/android"
        android:orientation="vertical"
        android:layout_width="fill_parent"
        android:layout_height="fill_parent"
    >

    <Button
android:text="Start Game"
android:layout_width="wrap_content"
android:id="@+id/startgame"
android:layout_height="wrap_content"
android:layout_x="557dip"
android:layout_y="249dip"></Button>

    <TextView
android:layout_width="wrap_content"
android:layout_height="wrap_content"
android:text="When you are ready to begin this game, please click on the button above."
android:id="@+id/textView1"
android:layout_x="310dip"
android:layout_y="361dip"></TextView>

</AbsoluteLayout>
```

The `layout_x` and `layout_y` lines specify where the items are located. If you want to precisely determine where the button and text are, you can edit these values. You use the `id` tags to reference the objects in the code, as you do in the next section.

Responding to a Start Game Button Press

Now that you have a nice display to put up for the user, you need to make it interactive. It's critical to allow the player to quickly start the game. This is especially important for a returning player. Remember that if the person is coming back to your game, they expect to begin playing very quickly and don't want to see instructions or be hassled by intro videos.

To display your new layout and then let the user navigate to the real game, let's go back to `MainActivity.java`. Here you do a simple input test and then show the actual game. Originally, however, you need to put `Main.xml` as the view of the game rather than `GameView.java`. Follow these steps:

1. Open `MainActivity.java` in the editing pane of Eclipse.

2. Add the following `import` statement to the top of the file:

```
import android.widget.Button;
```

3. Change the onCreate() method for MainActivity.java so it looks like Listing 10-3. The bold portions are changed from your previous work. You have to import Android.view.View in order to make it work.

Listing 10-3. MainActivity.java

```
@Override
public void onCreate(Bundle savedInstanceState) {
    super.onCreate(savedInstanceState);

    mGameView = new GameView(this);

    setContentView(R.layout.main);

    mSensorManager = (SensorManager)getSystemService(SENSOR_SERVICE);
    mAccelerometer = mSensorManager.getDefaultSensor(Sensor.TYPE_ACCELEROMETER);


    final Button button = (Button) findViewById(R.id.startgame);
    button.setOnClickListener(new View.OnClickListener() {
        public void onClick(View v) {

            setContentView(mGameView);
        }
    });

}
```

The first setContentView() tells the app to load main.xml as the layout. The button section listens for a click of the button. Once that happens, you call another setContentView() to show GameView on the screen. This is the simple method you use to initialize the game.

When you're assigning the value of the button, you use the function findViewById; and as the argument, you use the id of the button. This is the reason you make the button id something that can easily be identified as the item that starts the game.

4. Run the game, and you're presented with your welcome screen. Continue by pushing the Start Game button, and the application functions as normal.

Congratulations: you've finally finished the code portion of the book! The next section deals with doing the final compilation of the game and preparing to distribute it. You're getting closer to sharing your creation with other users.

Packaging the Game

You must take care of several things before the game is completed and ready to publish. This section goes over how you clean the code and finally compile the product into an APK file that is ready for distribution. An APK is the packaging that contains all of the game code, images, and resources.

Follow these steps:

1. The first order of business is to remove any `Log.d` statements in the code. I usually perform a global find and replace to delete them. You don't want a retail version to waste processing power sending our debug warnings.

2. You must fix the version of the code in the Android manifest file. Locate this file by going to the root of the `HarborDefender` folder and opening `AndroidManifest.xml`. The code should be similar the markup shown in Listing 10-4.

Listing 10-4. `AndroidManifest.xml`

```xml
<?xml version="1.0" encoding="utf-8"?>
<manifest xmlns:android="http://schemas.android.com/apk/res/android"
     package="com.gameproject.harbordefender"
     android:versionCode="1"
     android:versionName="1.0">
  <uses-sdk android:minSdkVersion="11" />

  <application android:icon="@drawable/icon" android:label="@string/app_name">
     <activity android:name=".MainActivity"
             android:label="@string/app_name">
       <intent-filter>
          <action android:name="android.intent.action.MAIN" />
          <category android:name="android.intent.category.LAUNCHER" />
       </intent-filter>
     </activity>

  </application>
</manifest>
```

Notice the bold portions. You can set your own version code and version name, but it's customary, because this is your first game, to use 1.0 as the version. Also ensure that the minimum SDK version is 11.

3. Choose File > Export in Eclipse.

4. Select Export Android Application as the type of export you would like to perform.

5. On the next page, enter the name of your final project: **Harbor Defender**.

6. You must create a keystore, which is required to protect the security of your application and is used as an identifier by the Android app market. Select Create New Keystore as shown in Figure 10-3, and use the Browse button to open a window that lets you place the file in a folder.. Type the file name as something like **harbordefenderkey**, and accept the default location.

Figure 10-3. The prompt to generate a key

7. Create a unique and difficult password for your own protection, as shown in Figure 10-3.

8. Fill out the Key Creation page shown in Figure 10-4 with the applicable information. (The figure shows how I completed it.) The password can be the same as the one that you used on the previous page.

Figure 10-4. Filling out the developer information

    9.   The next page is the last. Click Browse, and type **HarborDefender** as the APK destination. Close the dialog box, and finish the process.

    That's it—you've finished the project. The next section handles how you get this project into the Application Market and into the hands of consumers. You also cover how to best market and work on your presence in the crowded app market.

Deploying the Game

I hope you're satisfied with your game and confident that others will love it as well. This section covers how to work with Android App Market. You discover how applications are uploaded as well as the fundamentals of marketing and pricing. With this information, you can go back to making even more applications for sale.

    To get started, look at Figure 10-5, which shows the homepage of the Android App Market at `https://market.android.com/`.

Figure 10-5. The Android App Market

On this page, owners of Android mobile devices as well as tablets can download and purchase apps. Of special note is the tab that says Featured Tablet Apps. Android is making a large push to attract buyers of tablets, so it separates the apps that are designed specifically for tablets from those for phones. This is fantastic news for you because you face much less competition.

There is a lot of freedom when it comes to how the programs are offered. You can set a price for your app for any amount between $1 and $200 or give it away for free. When a customer buys it, you pocket 70% of the sale; the rest goes to the cost of sending the app to the device. Google doesn't take any portion of the proceeds, but the device makers and the online distributors are paid to handle the transaction much like a credit-card company charges a business for each transaction. iPhone and iPad apps give the developer only 60% of the revenue, so in this sense, Android has yet another advantage over the Apple App Store.

Fifty-seven percent of the apps on the Android market are free. Competing application stores have a much lower percentage of free apps. The implication for you is that you must be aware that programs that require users to pay must demonstrate superior quality and provide many hours of playing time.

You now know the basics of the market for apps. You must create an account with the Android App Market in order to see your own creations available. The next section covers how to make an account and upload your first app.

Opening a Google Developer Account

Nothing makes an application developer more pleased than to see their work in the hands of others. Here you create your Android App Market account and release your program to the world:

1. Go to https://market.android.com/. At the very bottom of the screen, click Developers.

2. Select the option to Publish Apps.

3. Sign in to your Google Account, or create a new one. You should create a new account just for your app business, to separate it from your regular e-mail or Google+ activities.

4. The next screen is shown in Figure 10-6. Fill it out with accurate and professional information. If you don't have a web site, that's okay, but you probably want one.

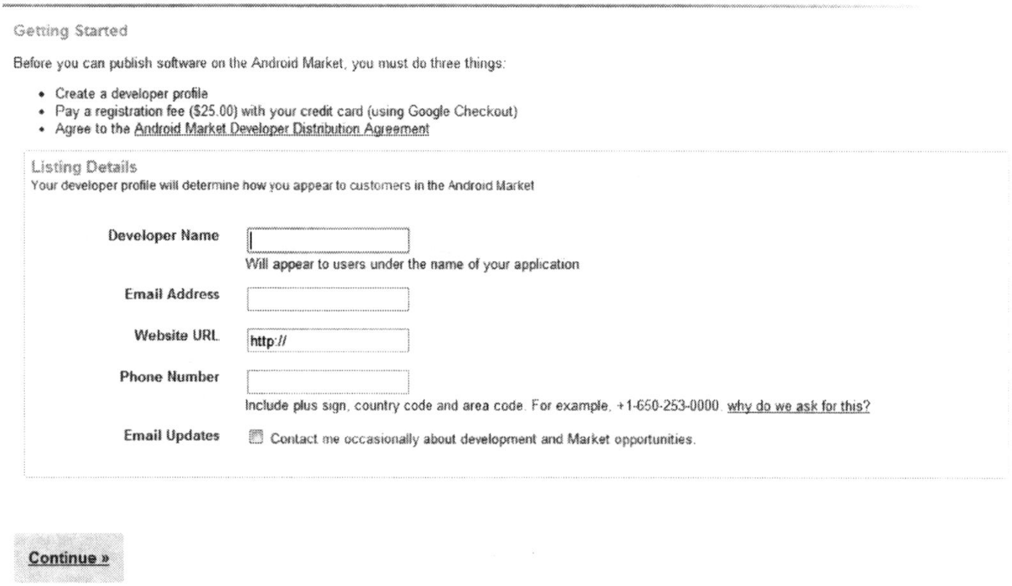

Getting Started

Before you can publish software on the Android Market, you must do three things:

- Create a developer profile
- Pay a registration fee ($25.00) with your credit card (using Google Checkout)
- Agree to the Android Market Developer Distribution Agreement

Listing Details
Your developer profile will determine how you appear to customers in the Android Market

Developer Name [   ]
Will appear to users under the name of your application

Email Address [   ]

Website URL [http://]

Phone Number [   ]
Include plus sign, country code and area code. For example, +1-650-253-0000. why do we ask for this?

Email Updates ☐ Contact me occasionally about development and Market opportunities.

Continue »

Figure 10-6. Creating your Android App Market Account

5. You're prompted to pay the registration fee. This is $25 and must be paid through Google Checkout.

When the registration is complete, you have a profile of sorts for your account. You can do a variety of things, from adding a Google Checkout account so you can get payments, to uploading an app.

Now you're ready to upload your game to Google Market.

Uploading a Game to Google Market

Although most developers want to sell their apps, this section covers the way to upload your app to the public free of charge. If you want to receive payments and charge for your work, go to this amazing guide about the market: www.google.com/support/androidmarket/developer/bin/topic.py?topic=15866.

Before you can complete the simple process to upload your game, you must have several items ready, including the following:

- The APK file that contains the app

- Two nice screenshots of the app that highlight its features

- A high-resolution icon that users select to play your game

Uploading the game is a simple proposition. At your online Developer Console, click Upload App. Here you go through a wizard that asks for the items just listed. Locate the files in the directory where you stored them.

It's critical to have an attractive screenshot and description as well as any additional diagrams that you would like to display; your success will be related to how much users are attracted to your game. The next section looks at how to prepare for the greatest possible success in the marketplace.

Marketing Your Game

Marketing your app involves exposing your product to the greatest number of people. If you've created a decent game, then people will buy it if they get the chance to see it. The first issue is how to make your app stand out. Unlike in the App Store for iPads and iPhones, Android programs can be downloaded from any web site, not just the official Google Market. This means developers with web sites of their own have a much easier time selling their products, because they aren't confused with the plethora of similar apps in the Market. Users can come directly to their site and see videos, graphics, and explanations of programs that aren't possible in the short description displayed at the Android Market.

Take advantage of this fact by creating your own web site and funneling potential buyers to it. Making a Facebook page or Twitter account can also generate increased attention. Instead of pointing readers to your page on the Android App Market, send them to a page on your own web site where there is less confusion.

If you've done online marketing, you know how useful a mailing list can be. On your site, offer visitors the opportunity to sign up for updates about yours apps and free extras. This way, you can continue to engage them and convince them to buy your offerings even if they don't purchase immediately. Check out the site AWeber (`www.aweber.com/`), which offers a fantastic mailing system you can use to distribute newsletters to your users. It charges per month, but many marketers find that the customers gained from the newsletter more than cover the cost.

Finally, approach the issue of marketing by putting your company or game into more traditional or trusted media. Ask magazines that focus on technology to review it, or send information about it to online news sources. When you do this, make sure your game offers something very unique. Maybe the input controls are totally innovative, or the game takes place inside a zero-gravity chamber. Make the app newsworthy. This can also be done by your company as a whole. If, for example, the art in all your games comes from a famous painter, that's definitely be a unique story for a site to talk about.

All these techniques go back to a basic funnel approach used in advertising. It's illustrated in a variety of beginning marketing and public relations books, but it also needs to be included here. The more users you can engage and the longer you engage them, the more sales you make. Figure 10-7 shows how this works.

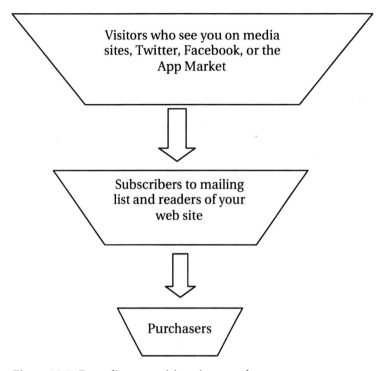

Figure 10-7. Funneling your visitors into purchasers

That is it for marketing tips. With some trial and error, you'll find the ways that work best for you. I have found that success in the App Market is rarely achieved on your first or even second game. You must stick with it and build anticipation and excitement about your offerings before striking gold.

Summary

Congratulations! You've completed the book. You went from discovering what Android is and how to program in it, to writing a complete game, to putting your work into the App Market.

This has been a fun and interesting book to write, and I hope you enjoyed it as well. Working on a technology that is so rapidly advancing can be both daunting and invigorating; ideally, this book has given you some idea about how to create your own games for Android tablets.

With Android's past success and its bright future, I am sure that the demand for better games for tablets will continue for a long time. Make sure you're there to catch this exciting wave.

APPENDIX A

Testing Android Games on a Real Device

If you're going to make games for an Android tablet, you definitely need to test them on the real thing. Android has a built-in way to do this that eliminates many of the hurdles that developers went through in the past to test their creations on videogame consoles and other mobile platforms. The marketplace for apps has very little tolerance for programs that have bugs or issues that could easily have been fixed during product testing.

This appendix guides you through a quick process to set up your tablet for testing. To follow along, you need an Android 3.0 tablet. There are many tablets on the market as I write this, with more arriving weekly, so it's impossible to list all of them. When I choose a device, I rarely look for the state-of-the-art tablet, but rather for the one that is most popular. If most people use the device that you use, then your results will be similar to those of the majority of your users.

Choose a tablet with a widely recognized brand name and a large following. If you have friends with tablets, you should test your applications on all of them. The process described here doesn't take long, so you should have no trouble doing this.

Because you're going to be debugging, the hardware interface requires that you specify your application as *debuggable*. You do this by setting a parameter in AndroidManifest.xml, the Android manifest file. When you look at your project folder in the Eclipse project explorer, you don't see the manifest file in it. Figure AppA-1 shows where to find this file.

Figure AppA-1. Android manifest file

You add a very simple parameter to the XML that defines the project as a debuggable program. Listing AppA-1 contains the code for the entire manifest, with the part that you must insert bolded.

Listing AppA-1. Android Manifest File

```
<?xml version="1.0" encoding="utf-8"?>
<manifest xmlns:android="http://schemas.android.com/apk/res/android"
    package="com.gameproject.firstapp"
    android:versionCode="1"
    android:versionName="1.0">
  <uses-sdk android:minSdkVersion="11" />

  <application android:icon="@drawable/icon" android:label="@string/app_name"
android:debuggable="true">

      <activity android:name=".Main"
            android:label="@string/app_name">
        <intent-filter>
          <action android:name="android.intent.action.MAIN" />
          <category android:name="android.intent.category.LAUNCHER" />
        </intent-filter>
      </activity>

  </application>
</manifest>
```

The next step varies a little from device to device. Google recommends going to the Application folder on the tablet, then going to the Development folder, and selecting USB Debugging. If this doesn't work for your tablet, do a quick search to find out how to turn on this type of debugging.

Now you need a driver for your specific USB device. This isn't the same as the one you may have installed when you connected the tablet to your computer for regular use. You need to choose one from the list of USB drivers on Google's Android developer page: http://developer.android.com/sdk/oem-usb.html. The process to install these is easy enough.

Take for example the Motorola tablet, which I own. I clicked the link to go to Motorola's homepage for developer drivers. Because I run my programs on a 64-bit version of Windows, I chose the latest handset USB driver. (Whether tablets are handsets is arguable, but the drivers are the same.) I followed the setup process and was ready to go.

■ **Note** If you're developing on a Macintosh computer, you don't need to worry about USB drivers: you're all set. Linux users, however, have a bit of work on their hands. For more information, check out the official Android documentation about setting up a device for development:

http://developer.android.com/guide/developing/device.html#setting-up.

If you follow these directions correctly, you can now test your programs on the device. Go to Eclipse, and run the program as usual. Instead of defaulting to the emulator, you should be presented with a choice between the device you added and the emulator. Select the device that you plugged in, and you can interact with your app the way your users will.

Pay careful attention to the fact that some applications only work on a physical device. These include apps that rely on accelerometer data or Bluetooth connections.

Index

CPSIA information can be obtained at www.ICGtesting.com
Printed in the USA
LVOW112011211211

260615LV00005B/79/P

9 781430 238522